Spy Rock Memories

Larry Livermore

Don Giovanni Records

ISBN: 978-0-9891963-0-7
e-ISBN: 978-0-9891963-1-4

Cover art: Gabrielle Bell
Cover design and lettering: Nolen Strals
Interior design: Doan Buu
Author photo: Christopher Ernst

To the people of Iron Peak, Spy Rock, and the Emerald Triangle: There were times we didn't get along, when we didn't understand or appreciate each other as much as we could have, but you were always on my mind—and in my heart.

one

My first trip up Spy Rock Road must have been sometime late in the summer of 1980. Jeff, my recently acquired brother-in-common-law, had bought a house and some land in the mountains of Northern California, and was planning to start a new life there with my sister and her two kids. Until, that is, he got involved in a misunderstanding with the authorities back east. Something, if memory serves me well, about a trunk load of marijuana.

Prevented from leaving the state by terms of his probation, he asked if I would keep an eye on the property until he was able to travel again. Eager for an excuse to get out of San Francisco for a couple of days, I agreed to drive up and have a look around.

"Cross the Golden Gate Bridge and drive north for about three hours," he told me. "The road where you turn off is just past a little town called Laytonville." It seemed as though I must have passed that way once or twice in my travels, but once I got beyond Healdsburg, everything looked completely unfamiliar.

At the Mendocino County line, the highway took a sudden swerve into rugged mountainous terrain, leaving behind the palm and orange trees that basked in Cloverdale's sultry valley heat. Pulling off for gas at Ukiah, the county seat and principal (read: only) city, I took a quick look at my surroundings, thought, "What a dump," and jumped back on the road.

Willits, not having yet turned into the unsightly several-miles-long strip mall it is today, struck me as a cute little town with considerable promise, boasting tree-lined streets, a pleasant city park, and at least a couple of decent-looking restaurants and cafes. I was expecting something similar of Laytonville, another 23 miles up the road. To say I was disappointed would be the understatement of the year, if not the decade.

It wasn't really a town at all, at least not what I thought of as a town. More like a ramshackle aggregation of two—no, back then there were three—gas stations, two stores (three, if you counted the liquor store), a couple of restaurants, a bar, and a church, sprawled alongside an unappealing, mostly treeless and sun-blanched stretch of Highway 101.

If forced to choose, I would have picked the Laytonville Inn as one of the classier buildings, if only because it had two stories, an Old West look, and was built out of wood instead of cinder block. A sign touted the virtues of its "famous Logger Burger," which sounded vaguely exotic to a city slicker like myself. Not sufficiently exotic to get me in the door, but enough to let me know I was really in the country now.

The temperature was in the low 90s, which, I would learn, was a mild summer day by Laytonville standards. Accustomed as I was to Bay Area weather, it felt like the Mojave Desert. I picked up some supplies at Geiger's General Store, the first general store I'd ever seen, other than in a movie or TV show. The fellow in front of me, in full cowboy regalia (boots and hat, anyway; he lacked a six-shooter), was buying a box of ammo. Everything he said began with "Yes, ma'am," "No, ma'am," or "I reckon."

Having been told there wouldn't be any more gas stations once I left Laytonville, I filled up the tank before taking a quick spin around town to make sure I hadn't missed anything. My tour was made just about worthwhile by the 12-foot-high wooden Indian standing guard over the Chief Drive-in and

Laundromat, home, the sign proclaimed, to the legendary Warrior Burger.

Northern California in the dying days of summer is not always the most picturesque of places, especially if you gauge your rural landscapes by their greenery. There was no short-age of trees, true, but they provided a feeble counterpoint to the fields and hillsides that faded beneath the unrelenting gaze of the sun from pale yellow into a lifeless and dispiriting brown. By that time of year the land itself begins to feel weary, able to do little more than stretch out and wait for autumn's renewing rains.

I continued north, as I'd been instructed, for exactly 8.9 miles. Just as I began to wonder if I'd misread my odometer, the highway dropped abruptly into a shady ravine. Halfway down the hill my eyes alighted on the sign I'd been watching for. Spy Rock Road, it read. An arrow pointed to the right, up into the hills.

I'd been looking forward to getting off the highway, imagining that once I did, I'd be wending my way through lush, cool forests, but Spy Rock was, if anything, hotter and drier than Highway 101. And dusty. I don't think I'd ever seen so much dust in my life. Within minutes my windshield was so dirty that I had trouble seeing where I was going.

Even at normal speeds, cars left billowing roostertails in their wake. In light of the hairpin turns and treacherous gravel surfaces, anything more than 20 or 25 mph felt dangerous, and the whole way up the mountain I never made it out of second gear. There wasn't much traffic, but most of the cars I did encounter were in a much bigger hurry than I was.

Periodically I'd pull over to let an aggressive tailgater pass, only to have to wait several more minutes for the dust cloud to clear. As I tentatively rounded one dizzying curve, I had to slam on the brakes to avoid a head-on collision with a seemingly out-of-control truck straight out of the *Beverly Hillbillies* by way of *Mad Max*.

Half an hour and 5.9 miles later, I reached the ridge, approximately 4,000 feet above sea level, hugging the northwest flank of Iron Peak. Here I was supposed to look for some sort of driveway that would take me up another small hill to the house. When I finally found it, I pulled off and sat clutching the steering wheel for several minutes before attempting to go any further.

The long slow crawl up the mountain had left my nerves so frazzled that I could think of only one possible reason for ever venturing onto Spy Rock Road again: to get the hell out of there and back to civilization. If you'd told me how many hundreds—if not thousands—of times I'd be up and down that road over the next couple of decades, I'd have begged you to just shoot me then and there.

My feelings changed—a bit—once I made it to the house, a quaint and quirky structure whose design owed as much to whimsy as it did to blueprints or planning codes. Nobody had been living there for the better part of a year; the smell of solitude mingled with that of the sun-baked paneling and floorboards that creaked and popped as I walked through the living room and into the rustic kitchen.

It was almost unbearably hot inside, but once I opened some windows, a cool breeze—there was almost always a cool breeze at that altitude—swept through the house, carrying with it the sounds and scents of softly stirring pine trees. A bird landed on the roof with a loud thud, causing me to nearly jump out of my skin. Rustling trees and random house noises notwithstanding, I don't think I had ever, in my entire life, been someplace so deafeningly, pervasively, almost frighteningly silent.

I wandered outside again, down the driveway, back to the

road I'd come in on. From the ridge I had an unobstructed view of the Yolla Bolly Mountains to the east and the Pacific Ocean to the west. To the north, across a deep and thickly forested canyon, rose an imposing cliff face of stark, jagged black rock. Directly in front of me sat the massive, hulking presence of Iron Peak, crowned with a fire lookout tower that, in the right light, looked almost like a pagoda.

In those days, before cell phones and satellite technology made human lookouts obsolete, someone was stationed in the tower all summer long. I decided to hike up there and soon found myself on a steep, unforgiving road that I wouldn't have dared attempt in a car. By the time I reached the summit, the afternoon sun was hanging low in the sky.

The guy manning the tower spotted me long before I made it to the top. When I was within hailing distance, he shouted an invitation to come upstairs and join him. We sat chatting, drinking coffee (augmented, if I'm not mistaken, by something a little stronger), and admiring the view that stretched some 75 miles in every direction.

The sun extinguished itself in the sea with a fleeting flurry of oranges, reds, and purples. Just like that, it was pitch black outside, and well past time for me to start back down the mountain. I could see lights at a few points far below, arrayed here and there along the sinuous curves of Highway 101. The tower itself was illuminated—barely—by a couple of solar-powered 12-volt fluorescents.

But their faint glow faded away before I'd made it 50 feet downhill. A few years later my eyes would have grown so used to the darkness that wandering through fields and forests in the midst of a moonless night would be second nature. But that first starlit journey down the mountain reduced me to abject terror.

I could see nothing but vague shadowy outlines, and had to more or less feel my way home. There was little margin for error. To my left the road clung tightly to the face of the mountain; on the right, it fell away into a steep cliff. The center of the road seemed like the right place to walk, or would have, if I hadn't been warned to watch out for the rattlesnakes that liked to lie there after dark, savoring the last bits of the day's warmth that lingered in the rocks and sand.

By the time I made it back to the house, it was past midnight. In the city, I might just be getting ready to go out for the evening, but here I was at a loss for what to do with myself. I strummed my guitar and sang a few songs by candlelight, got bored, and turned on a battery-powered radio that offered a mind-numbing variety of country music, news, and ranting talk show hosts from across the western United States. All of it, however, apart from one San Francisco station, faded in and out to the point of being nearly unlistenable.

I never thought about going to sleep. I couldn't have anyway, and not just because of all the coffee I'd been drinking. The life I'd led the past few years unfolded mostly at night. I'd typically get up between 4 and 6 in the afternoon and get to bed—if at all—somewhere around 8 or 10 in the morning. It wasn't the healthiest of lifestyles, I guessed, but I was used to it, and still young enough that it didn't seem to faze me.

Physically, that is. Mentally it was another story.

I privately suspected I was going a little crazy, which was a big part of the reason I'd jumped at the chance to get away from the city. In the 60s and early 70s, I'd been what you might call a sprouthead, awash in granola and Earth shoes, forever consulting the *I Ching* and babbling about horoscopes and "the vibes."

But then I'd succumbed to the cynicism that often arrives

with one's late 20s, exacerbated by the nihilism of punk rock, which I'd embraced as enthusiastically as I had the mystical hippie bullshit of the previous decade. The net result was that I had turned into one jaded bastard.

Was I looking for something to believe in? To live for, even? You wouldn't catch me admitting it, but something odd did happen on my second or third trip up Spy Rock. Yes, despite swearing I'd never drive up that road again, I did, and not entirely unwillingly. With my brother-in-common-law still ensnared by legal troubles back east, I wound up becoming his de facto caretaker, and even began, in some weird, ambivalent way, to look forward to my visits to this alien but intriguing land.

It was late March. A lush California spring was well underway down in the valleys, but winter still held a cold hard grip on Spy Rock. I'd been late getting away from the city, so it was long past dark by the time I reached the ridge. The moon flitted in and out of a cluster of windblown clouds, creating a chiaroscuro effect that, while hauntingly beautiful, felt just a bit unsettling.

As I rounded the final bend, the moon shook off the last of the clouds that had been dogging it. A sudden burst of light splashed across the north face of Iron Peak, which was dappled with splotches of near-luminous snow. I shivered as a strange notion popped into my head.

"A man could die up here if he wasn't careful."

I repeated the words out loud. For some reason, the idea had a certain seductive appeal. The mountain felt like a place where real life happened, where actions had consequences, where one had to make choices more crucial than what restaurant to eat at or what movie to see.

It was probably in that moment that the prospect of living

on Spy Rock made the subtle shift from fantasy to inevitability. I began coming up every month or two, and on Thanksgiving of 1981, I brought my new girlfriend along for the first time.

Anne and I were barely halfway up the mountain when it started snowing. If I'd had any sense, I would have turned around and headed back to the city. You don't spend long on Spy Rock without discovering that winter weather is not to be trifled with or taken lightly. But just then it seemed like a great adventure, so I plowed ahead, slipping and sliding all over the road in my wildly inappropriate Honda Prelude.

We made it to the ridge top somehow, just before the road became completely impassable. Leaving the car at the bottom of the driveway, we walked the last quarter mile through almost a foot of snow. I knew we were hopelessly stranded, but I assumed, with no particular grounds for doing so, that the snow would magically melt away before it was time to go home.

After a spectacular Thanksgiving dinner, we took a starry-eyed walk through a similarly spectacular winter landscape. Civilization and its discontents were a million miles away; with even our footsteps muffled by the newly fallen snow, the silence was all but absolute.

We sat up late, talking and dreaming by candlelight, and woke the following morning to find that a warm southerly breeze had sprung up, raising the temperature into the 60s and stripping snow from the mountainsides so quickly that by late afternoon we had no problem at all driving out of there and back down to the city.

When I next returned to Spy Rock, it was mid-January and I was on my own, Anne having shown no enthusiasm for a midwinter trek up the mountain. There was snow everywhere, but the road, while scary in spots, was mostly drivable. I was poking around the house, wondering if I had enough firewood to last the night, when I heard a car pull up outside.

Half curious, half alarmed—I'd never had a visitor at the house before and had no idea who it could be—I peeked stealthily out a back window. A smallish, bearded man stood eyeing my car suspiciously. He looked up, noted the smoke coming from my chimney, and nodded as though his suspicions had been confirmed.

I slipped on my boots, went out the front door, rounded the house, and came up behind him.

"Um, hello? Can I help you?"

"Hello," he answered. "What are you doing here?"

I was taken aback by his bluntness. As far as I could see, he was the one who should be explaining his presence. But though he was shorter than me by several inches, he had a muscular build and a manner suggesting he was not the sort of man I wanted to get belligerent with.

So I identified myself and explained the situation. The stranger's manner immediately softened. "My name is Udo," he said. "I built this house, and used to live here until I sold it to Jeff. I was hoping I might find him here." Apparently news of my brother-in-common-law's legal predicament hadn't yet reached him.

Then, in what I would come to learn was a near-universal gesture of mountain hospitality, he offered to smoke a joint with me.

I was still a semi-regular smoker in those days, but was totally unprepared for the power and intensity of Udo's marijuana, which seemed to have arrived straight from the Planet Blotto (something that would prove to be typical of most dope grown on Spy Rock). It was almost like being on LSD, but without the jagged, paranoid edge I often experienced when getting high in the city.

It felt, dare I say, more "organic" than my usual drug experiences. There was a sense not just of euphoria, but of being deeply connected to nature, the land, and this gnomish stranger, who regaled me with mind-boggling tales of mountain life, and hair-raising ones about his childhood and young adulthood in East Germany, from which he'd managed to escape through a series of plots and misadventures worthy of a spy thriller.

After recounting the bizarre chain of circumstances that had led a onetime Rhine River boat captain to become a self-employed carpenter in the Northern California wilderness, Udo invited me to dinner at the house he was building on "the other side of the mountain." Telling me to follow him, he jumped into his car and tore off as if he were merging into the fast lane of the Autobahn from Frankfurt to Düsseldorf.

It was the first time I'd ever driven past the ridge. As I soon discovered, the road took a turn (quite a few turns, actually) for the worse, plunging almost immediately downhill into an area of heavy snow. Before Udo's car disappeared from view, I could see its back end swaying from side to side as he slid into curves like a slalom skier. I gave up trying to catch him, and did my best to follow in the tracks he'd left while not winding up in a ditch or off a cliff.

No more than 15 or 20 minutes had passed, but it felt like I had driven halfway to the North Pole before I saw Udo again. He was standing at the side of the road, clapping his hands to keep warm. Pointing to a spot behind his car, he indicated I should pull in there.

"What happened?" he said. "I thought you changed your mind and decided not to come."

"I couldn't go fast enough to keep up with you. I was afraid I'd slide off the road."

"Nonsense. The trick to driving in these conditions is not to slow down."

Still recovering from what had felt like a near-death experience, I didn't see the point of arguing. "How much further is it to your house?" I asked.

"We're here! But we have to walk the last little bit because there's too much snow on the driveway."

We clambered up a steep hillside, following a barely visible path through thickets of bushes, trees, and the thorny remnants of last summer's blackberry vines. On reaching the crest I gasped, not just for air, but at the mind-stopping spectacle awaiting me there. Snow-topped mountains framed a panorama of rolling fields and forests that undulated their way to the bottom of the Eel River canyon.

Off to my right, at the bottom of a small hill and nestled in a grove of fir and pine trees, stood a two-story wooden house, smoke curling upward from its chimney. Two children were playing out front, tossing snowballs for their dog to chase. I felt like I was looking at a Christmas card come to life. It was one of the most beautiful sights I had ever seen.

Inside, more revelations awaited. The place where I'd been staying had its charming features, but in many ways remained a mere shell of a house. This was a real home. There were electric lights—dim ones, granted, powered by two small solar panels on the roof—and a fully equipped kitchen, where Josie, Udo's wife, was making dinner.

An upright piano occupied a prominent place in the living room, directly opposite the wood-burning stove. Sitting down to play a few tunes, I discovered that the walls and beams functioned as an extended sounding board, causing the piano notes to resonate from floor to ceiling and effectively turning the whole house into a musical instrument.

We lingered over dinner, talking for what must have been hours. Eventually the children got bored and went upstairs to their rooms. Around the time we were eating dessert, a crazy idea crept into my head. While the conversation drifted all over the map, alighting on a dozen or more subjects, this idea kept dancing around the edges of my consciousness, refusing to let go.

My first thought had been, "Wouldn't it be nice to live in a place like this?" That turned into, "Wouldn't it be nice to live in *this* place?" And then, finally, "Well, why not?"

The most obvious reason was that there was already a family living there. But if Udo had sold his previous home to Jeff and my sister, wasn't it possible he'd be willing to sell this one, too? Even if he'd told me an hour earlier that he meant it to be a permanent place for his family, and had no plans to move again?

In any event, it was an idiotic notion from start to finish. I'd never lived in the country. I didn't know anything about living in the country.

Cut firewood? Put snow chains on tires? Cope with trees falling on houses or roads blocked by landslides? I couldn't even manage minor household repairs; my girlfriend handled things like that or they didn't get done.

Besides, my whole life revolved around the city. If there weren't restaurants and bars and cafes and theaters practically at my doorstep, I didn't really see the point of living.

Still, I had to admit it was a pleasant fantasy to let roll around my head as we smoked our second or third after-dinner joint. I excused myself to use the bathroom, and it was there that the fateful die was cast.

Although Udo was still finishing the interior of the house, the bathroom was one room that was not only pretty much

18

done, but also represented the pinnacle of his craftsmanship. With half a dozen shades and textures of new and recycled wood, painted tiles, and a vintage tub and sink, it had the look and feel of a perfect little jewel box. Well, inasmuch as a bathroom is ever going to resemble a jewel box. By the time I returned to the dining room table, I had made my decision. I was going to buy this house and live here.

I'd never owned a house before, never seriously considered it. And while I thought I might be able to afford it, it would require pretty much every penny I had. What would I do for money after I bought it? Didn't matter. I wasn't going to let petty things like reason or logic intrude on my vision.

I casually asked Udo and Josie if they'd consider selling the property. While they were still reeling from this unexpected turn in the conversation, I offered them a sum of money that I guessed would leave them in no position to say no.

Even as this was happening, I knew it was one of the most insane things I'd ever done. The previous few years had been good for me financially, but not so good that I could afford to sink my life savings into a whim. I didn't even try to negotiate a lower price, partly out of fear Udo and Josie would say no, partly because I felt a little guilty about trying to buy their house out from under them.

It was like sky diving, I reasoned: once you make the decision to jump out of an airplane, you might as well go ahead and do it. Second, third, or fourth thoughts are not going to make the prospect look any more inviting.

And that, it turned out, was that. By the time I headed back to my side of the mountain, we'd shaken hands on the deal and I had the rest of the night to lie awake wondering what I'd done.

I knew I'd just bought the most beautiful house in the world, there was no doubt of that, but that house also happened to be located nine miles from the nearest paved road, five miles beyond the nearest power line or telephone.

I figured I could handle the isolation, and there wasn't any reason—well, no logical reason—I couldn't learn the necessary skills for surviving on and managing the 45 acres of land that came with it. But then another thought insinuated itself, one that made my blood run distinctly chilly, if not downright cold.

In all my musings and fantasies, I'd never stopped to think about Anne, who had only recently moved in with me. She was even more of a city person than I was, and was not likely to be thrilled with my unilateral decision to move to the backside of nowhere. The only question, I suspected, was how long it would take her to break up with me.

Though we'd only been together eight months, we had a pretty solid relationship, as serious as any I'd ever been involved in. I'd go so far as to say that marriage might have been in the cards. Didn't that kind of relationship mean you talked about stuff, made plans together, asked the other person's opinion instead of just doing whatever popped into your head?

Yes, this was true, I conceded. But I wasn't going to let it change my mind. I was pretty sure Anne would be hurt and angry that I hadn't consulted her, sure enough that I even manufactured a feeble excuse in advance: there were no phones on the mountain (true) and I'd had to make a decision on the spot (not even remotely true).

Where the conversation might go from there, I didn't know, and didn't want to speculate. If Anne decided not to come with me, I'd become a jolly old hermit, talking to the trees and the animals, living in harmony with nature, enjoying a pure and simple existence in complete and blissful solitude.

If I'd known the course my life was about to take, if I'd had the faintest idea what it would be like to live out here beyond the reach of society's civilizing constraints, if I'd had an inkling of the changes and challenges that would confront me, I'd have headed straight back to Josie and Udo's the next morning and tried to laugh off the whole affair with a "Wow, I was really high last night. I hope I didn't say anything too embarrassing."

But that was the key: I had no idea, no idea at all, not a single, solitary clue. Which is exactly how I bumbled my way into the greatest adventure of my life.

two

In my younger days, I liked to make up stories. If you wanted to be uncharitable, I guess you could have called them lies, but let's not split hairs. I managed to convince myself that this was an amusing, even charming habit, but I suspect most people did not share that opinion.

I didn't do it for personal gain—not usually, anyway—nor with the intention of permanently deceiving anyone. The point of the game was to convince someone that what I was saying was true—the more preposterous the better—then pull the rug out from under them with a, "No, just kidding."

It might be something implausible but innocuous like, "I ran into the mayor at a party the other day and she really liked my ideas about urban planning." Other times the "joke" could be more heavy-handed, along the lines of, "Hey, are you in trouble? The police were just here looking for you!"

Although we'd only met the previous spring, Anne was already well versed in this routine. Which probably explains why she didn't seem shocked or appalled when I casually mentioned I had bought some property on Iron Peak, and was planning to move there.

Instead of the "You did WHAT?" I was expecting, her reaction was along the lines of, "That's nice, dear. Did you remember to pick up some milk while you were out?" I assumed she was playing along with what she thought was another of my farfetched stories; her tune would change, I was sure, the minute she realized I wasn't making this up.

But she didn't break up with me, didn't suggest I was out of my ever-loving mind, didn't even complain that I hadn't talked this idea over with her in advance. She had her doubts and misgivings, but once she saw that I was serious, she said, "Of course I'm going with you. What made you think I wouldn't?"

One reason I'd thought she wouldn't was that Anne had only recently moved to the Bay Area, and, like many East Coast transplants, was completely enthralled with her new home. I'd been the same way when I arrived from Michigan in 1968. For many years afterward, I couldn't imagine wanting to live anywhere else.

In recent years, though, San Francisco had lost some of its charm for me, and my longstanding love affair with The City was all but shattered one summer night shortly after Anne and I began dating. Having seen a movie at a little artsy-type theater in an alley off Polk Street, we were walking back to my brother's apartment on Russian Hill, where we were house sitting while he was in Mexico. As we headed up Bush Street, a carload of guys rolled by.

"Hey, faggots!" they shouted.

Anne had short hair and a slightly androgynous look, but was not someone you'd normally mistake for a guy, homosexual or otherwise. And I thought I should have been absolved, at least for the moment, of looking like a "faggot," if only on grounds that I was holding hands with a girl.

Not the case, unfortunately. Anne rolled her eyes the way she did when someone or something struck her as absurd—I wouldn't be surprised if she stuck her tongue out at them, too—and we kept walking. They came back around the block, cruising slowly past us. This time they were brandishing 2x4s, banging them loudly on the sides of their car and pointing at us to indicate that they might like to do something similar to our heads.

We ran into a corner store and hung out for a while. After looking out the window several times and seeing no sign of our tormenters, we started up the hill again, but hadn't made it half a block before they were back.

We ducked into alleys, hid behind hedges, tore up and down hills for the next half hour, but couldn't shake them. Finally, we were within sight of my brother's place. Another 50 yards and we'd be safe, but those 50 yards were up a ridiculously steep hill, one frequently used by filmmakers in those hair-raising San Francisco car chase sequences.

It looked like the coast was clear, but just as we were ready to make a dash for it, the car came careening around the corner and we were trapped.

"Downhill!" Anne shouted. "Run downhill!"

It didn't make sense. Downhill would take us away from my brother's house, not toward it. And what made her think we could outrun a car?

But the urgency in her voice—plus the fact that I didn't have any better ideas—led me to do as she said. We tore off down Taylor Street; the car wheeled around and came after us, picking up speed until it looked about to go airborne.

Just as it caught up with us, Anne shouted again, "Now go uphill!"

Turning on a dime, we raced toward home and I saw the method in her madness: the driver slammed on his brakes, but he'd built up so much momentum that it carried him the rest of the way down the hill. By the time he could stop and find a place to turn around, we were safely inside.

It wasn't the first scary experience I'd had on the streets of San Francisco. I'd once had a kid stick a gun in my stomach at the corner of Church and Market, and only recently a teenage rat pack had tried to yank open the doors of our car while Anne and I waited at a stoplight in the Western Addition.

But tonight, I decided, was the last straw.

"I've had it with this town," I announced. "I'm going to move somewhere and start my own city."

At the time I wasn't necessarily thinking of moving to the country, or anywhere in particular. I just had this vague fantasy, dating back to early childhood, of getting away, of finding some place devoid of troublesome people, where things were done the right way (aka my way). I entertained thoughts about a nuclear apocalypse or alien invasion that would kill off everyone but me (I might, if I was feeling magnanimous, let a few friends live).

In my darker moments (we're talking about a 6 or 8-year-old child, remember), I'd daydream about getting my hands on some heavy weaponry and launching an assault on school, church, playground, anywhere that my enemies—who, as a rule, included somewhere between 99.5% and 100% of the world's population—might be lurking.

It never occurred to me that these were strange thoughts for a young child to be having. Nor did I ever think that, should my fantasies come true, I might find it lonely being the last living boy on earth. On the contrary, a world without people seemed like paradise. I could help myself to anything I wanted, wander through the world doing exactly as I pleased, eat and drink whatever I liked, get up and go to bed whenever I chose.

I'd like to say I'd matured beyond this point by the time I reached my 30s, but it wouldn't be entirely true. As recently as 1979 I'd written a science fiction novel based on one of my time-honored premises: a plutonium leak causing the extinction of, well, basically everyone on earth that I didn't like. The handful of survivors made their final stand in, as it happened, the mountains of Northern California.

When I wrote that book, I had never set foot in or laid eyes on those mountains. All I knew was that they were where marijuana came from. I imagined them being filled with old-fashioned hippies living in harmony with nature. Or something like that, along with some quasi-mysticism and the occasional ritual murder.

Minus the ritual murder, it was the sort of life I now looked forward to. Everything would be, as the hippies used to say, groovy. No unpleasant situation or unwelcome stranger would dare intrude. A new, better-designed Eden. My own private Larryland. La-la land would have been more like it.

Anne and I set out for our new home on March 1, 1982, my little Honda—as ludicrously unsuited for Spy Rock's bone-breaking back roads as we two city slickers were for the rigors of mountain life—loaded to the gills with everything we thought we might need to survive in the wilderness. Most of it was junk that would have been more appropriate for some weekend poking around in a backyard suburban garden.

We didn't pack much—hell, we didn't own much—in the way of winter clothing. Bay Area temperatures seldom dropped below freezing, and by the beginning of March, spring was already in full effect. Our first night on the mountain found us huddled around the stove trying, with only partial success, to keep warm. Outside, patches of snow and still-bare trees seemed to make it clear that spring was nowhere in sight.

But in the morning the sun was shining brightly, and continued to do so day after day for our first few weeks on the mountain. The last bits of snow vanished, and splotches of green appeared, spreading like inkblots until whole hillsides were transformed into rich velvety carpets.

Udo had warned me that I'd need to cut more firewood; the pile he'd left would barely last a couple days during a real cold snap. But that hardly seemed likely now. Daytime temperatures routinely reached into the 70s. If we lit a fire at all, it was only a small one to take the chill off mornings and evenings.

Instead of cutting wood, my energy went into planting trees and flowers. At least twice a week I'd drive down to Laytonville or Willits, where I'd fill the car with rootstocks, fertilizer, and hundreds of pounds of soil, all of which had to be carried up and over the hill on my back. As instructed by my *How To Grow Productive Fruit Trees* manual, I dug holes—3' by 3' by 4'—using a pickaxe to smash through slabs of rock that had the temerity to plant themselves in the spot I knew was just right for an apple tree.

Between half and two thirds of the land was covered in forest, a mixture of fir, pine, oak, madrone, manzanita, and the occasional maple or cedar. It had been logged in the past, though for the most part not clear-cut. It was mainly the giant Douglas firs and Ponderosa pines that had been taken; their decaying stumps, five, six, sometimes even eight feet across, hinted at how dramatically this landscape must have been altered.

Above and to the east of the house, and stretching out far below, were expanses of grassy hillside. It was there that I put in most of my fruit trees. On the north face of the property there was another such area. Covered by mud and rocks in some spots, grass in others, it looked as though a devastating landslide had torn through it at some time in the not too distant past.

In a fit of hubris, I decided I would single-handedly reclaim this slope, planting hundreds of fir and pine seedlings that I bought from the local Forest Service office. About ten of them would survive that first summer.

By the last week of March I had built up muscles I never knew I had. Working shirtless much of the time had given me an almost tropical-style tan. When, in the midst of my labors, I'd stop for a breather, I'd often feel all but overwhelmed by the beauty that surrounded me.

Wildflowers were bursting into bloom, as were buds on the almond, peach, cherry, and plum trees. Standing there dripping with sweat in the midday sun that seemed to grow warmer and more intense every day, I reflected that if the Eskimos really did have 28 words for snow (I'm pretty sure they don't, but it was one of those things you always heard people say), I'd need more than that to describe the multifarious shades of green that came cascading over the land for as far as the eye could see.

If it was already this beautiful in March, I could scarcely imagine what I had to look forward to in May or June. Unwilling to wait that long, I brought home flats of spring and summer flowers every time I went to town. I had become one of Weathertop Nursery's best customers, but that didn't stop young Jordan Celso, the owners' son, from observing that it might be a tad early for some of the plants I was picking out.

"I'm pretty sure we're done with winter for this year," I told him.

"Only fools and foreigners predict the weather around these parts," he amiably replied, leaving me scratching my head and wondering what exactly he could have meant by that.

There are certain times of year when, because of temperature inversions, it's colder in the valley where Laytonville sits than up in the mountains. This was one of those times. In town there'd be a frosty nip in the air, but with every mile I traveled up Spy Rock, the temperature would rise another five or ten degrees. The only problem with this summerlike weather was that we still needed a little more rain to replenish the streams and wells before the dry season set in.

But day after day saw not a cloud on the horizon, let alone a hint of precipitation. It stayed that way for almost the entire month. By then Anne and I were beginning to feel like old hands at country living. Vestiges of our urban selves remained: for example, Anne refused to let me go to sleep until I'd gone out and locked the car doors, even though, locals assured us, we'd be more likely to have an encounter with Bigfoot than a random burglar or prowler.

There'd come a time—not so many years down the line—when I wouldn't even bother locking the house for days or weeks at a time. But during those first months, a crackling twig, a mysterious screech or yowl, even the thunk of a pinecone landing on the roof, would have me reaching for the shotgun to repel a home invasion.

Udo and his family visited now and then, but we saw little of our other neighbors. Sometimes we'd hear a chain saw or truck engine revving up in the distance, and once in a while somebody shouting or singing, but most of the time the only sounds were those of nature. The one constant was the roar of the creeks, a small one at the bottom of our land, and a huge one—especially at that time of year—just over the hillcrest, each carrying a winter's worth of rain and snow melt down into the Eel River Canyon.

Frank, who lived a mile down the hill, was one of our closest neighbors. We met him early one morning when he came barreling up the road just as we were pulling out of our driveway. Sliding to a halt in a flurry of loose gravel, he rolled down his window and shouted an exuberant "Howdy!" before lighting a joint and thrusting it in our direction.

"Um, thanks," I said, "but it's like 7:30 in the morning. Kind of early for me."

He looked at me as if I were an imbecile. Then his face softened; you could see he was trying to make allowances, to take into consideration that I was, after all, a city slicker who wasn't used to mountain ways.

"I'm on my second one already!" he crowed. "I've got errands to run, so I rolled up a few to tide me over." He showed me a metal cigarette case containing nine or ten joints.

"How long were you planning to be gone?" I asked.

"All morning! Maybe part of the afternoon!"

A word about dope: it wasn't that I was against it. I used it fairly often, though nothing like Anne, who was a daily smoker. And I was aware that marijuana growing was a major source of income around there, though I hadn't yet figured out it was pretty much the only source.

I actually romanticized the notion of outlaw growers carving out a niche for themselves and their families where they could live off the grid, disconnected from mainstream society. But it wasn't something I necessarily wanted to be a part of.

Ideally I would have preferred to have no marijuana at all on our property, but we agreed that Anne could put in a small garden for her own use. It seemed like a reasonable compromise. But I remained determined not to become a grower myself—a resolution I was able to stick to for the first several years.

March 26th brought a sudden turn in the weather. The sun barely made it over the horizon before disappearing into a bank of clouds that had come barging in over the ridge. The temperature dropped sharply, and we had to keep a fire going all day.

I was not at all happy about that, because it meant having to find more firewood. Until now, because of the long spell of mild weather, I'd made do by picking up scraps around the land and occasionally breaking out the hand saw to cut up some smallish branches.

I'd resisted getting a chain saw—I was probably the only homesteader on the mountain who didn't own one—partly because I detested the noise and fumes they gave off, and partly because they scared me half to death. I had this quixotic notion that, through careful husbandry and a little extra work, I could get by like the old-time pioneers had, doing everything by hand.

Which had worked just fine until now. I'd decided this firewood thing was not as tough a business as people made it out to be. But my faith was shaken when I woke up the next morning and was able to see my breath inside the house. Overnight the temperature had dropped into the upper 20s. Around 4 o'clock that afternoon, when I realized the stove was devouring my firewood supply faster than I could replenish it, I admitted defeat, and announced that I was going into Laytonville to buy a chain saw.

Anne urged me to wait until morning, when I'd have time to run some other errands, but I wanted to get it over with, and, knowing that the store closed at 5, jumped into the car with only minutes to spare. A harsh, biting wind had sprung up, and the sullen, angry stratus layer that had obscured the sky all day seemed to be sinking lower, as if it were bent on swallowing up the mountain.

Bailey's Logging Supplies, located in a rustic clapboard structure that a couple years later would become home to the Laytonville Post Office, was the kind of place people like me tended to avoid. Owner Bill Bailey was said to be none too sympathetic toward newcomers, especially those suspected of hippie inclinations.

Despite the rumors, the clerks were nothing but courteous and helpful, even though I was their last customer of the day and they were anxious to close up and get home themselves. Hadn't I heard a major winter storm was supposed to be headed our way?

I hadn't, actually, and didn't take their warnings too seriously. After all, it was almost April. In the unlikely event that we got some snow, it would probably come and go as quickly as it had that first Thanksgiving on Spy Rock.

I pulled out of Bailey's parking lot a little after closing time, the proud—if slightly reluctant—owner of an orange Husqvarna chain saw with a 20-inch bar ("Anything more than 24 inches and a guy is just showing off," the salesman assured me). It had cost me a lot of money, more than I'd planned on spending, but the guys at Bailey's had advised me well. It was exactly the right piece of equipment for our needs, and very well might have saved our lives.

I picked up a few groceries at Geiger's and headed up the mountain, hoping to make it home before dark so I could try out my new saw and get some wood in for the night. The windshield stayed dry most of the way up Spy Rock, but by the time I got to the ridge, I was driving in the clouds.

It was slow going, and turning on my headlights didn't help at all; if anything, their reflected glare made it even harder to see. As I reached the end of the ridgeline and started my descent toward home, the first snowflakes began to fly.

The drive from the top of the ridge to the bottom of my driveway usually took between ten and twenty minutes, depending how much of a hurry I was in. That was all the time it took for the snow to thicken and accumulate to the point where I was barely able to stay on the road or, for that matter, find it.

Rather than drive all the way to the house, I left the car at the bottom of the driveway, as I'd been advised by more experienced locals. The roads would get plowed sooner or later, but unless you made prior arrangements and paid someone a hefty chunk of change, your driveway could stay snowed in until spring.

But it already *was* spring, I silently protested as I trudged over the hill and down to the house in almost total darkness. Anne greeted me at the front door; she was her usual ebullient self, but I could tell she'd been worried I might not make it back before the snow made travel impossible.

She had the kitchen stove going full blast as she cooked up a feast to celebrate what we assumed might be a day or two of being snowed in. It kept that room warm, but a chill hung over the rest of the house. The fire in the wood stove was just limping along, and we had to ration our few remaining sticks and scraps to keep it going as long as we could before heading upstairs to bed.

I woke up around 8 am, but assumed it was much earlier because of the gloomy half-light that filled the room. It took me a minute or two to realize what else was unusual: the almost deathly quiet. No bird calls, no wind sighing through the trees, none of the creaks, cracks, and groans that constantly emanate from a wooden house in the country.

Most disconcerting of all was the temperature: absolutely freezing. Normally a few hot coals would have survived from the previous night's fire, enough to give off a little warmth and to spring back to life as soon as fresh fuel was added.

Not today. There wasn't a spark to be found; the stove was cold as a coffin.

"I'd better get some wood before we do anything else," I told Anne. Opening the front door, I found myself facing a chest-deep wall of snow. I'd left a few pieces of firewood lying not too far from the house, but the only way I was going to get them now was to dig my way there.

Which was how I spent the first half of my morning, painstakingly—and painfully—shoveling a path to the meager remains of my woodpile. By the time I got there, the storm had filled in my path and I had to dig my way back again. In the afternoon I repeated this process.

By nightfall I'd spent eight, maybe ten hours digging through snow, picking up, cutting, and hauling wood. All that activity kept me warm personally, but it wasn't doing much for the house. The wood I'd been able to retrieve was wet, burned poorly, and gave off little heat. At best, we were able to keep the area immediately in front of the stove—maybe ten square feet—at a livable temperature.

We dragged our mattress down from the bedroom and set up camp in the living room. The battery pack kept our lights going for the first couple days, but with the solar panels that charged it buried deep beneath the snow, they gradually faded away until we were living mostly by candlelight. Fortunately, our refrigerator was propane-powered—not that keeping things cold was likely to be a problem anytime soon.

Maintaining our water supply was a bit more worrisome. We had to leave a tap running at night to keep the pipes from freezing, but that could only go on so long before the tank ran dry. If it came to that, of course, we could always subsist on melted snow, so we'd be looking at more of an inconvenience than a disaster.

At least we weren't going to starve. Neighbors had recommended we keep a month's supply of food on hand in case of emergencies like this. It would have lasted a month, too, if we hadn't overeaten a bit during the first few days, when we assumed the blizzard was a freakish occurrence that was bound to blow over soon.

As it turned out, the storm went on for twelve days. Even after it stopped snowing, the five-plus feet that had been dumped on us showed no sign of melting away. For the first week, I was trapped within a 150-foot radius of the house, which was about as far as I could dig my way out and back again. Within that area, I had to find and cut enough wood to keep us from freezing.

I hadn't yet learned that green wood—i.e., from living trees—was hard to burn and didn't give off much heat. Struggling to keep my footing in the snow, sometimes barely able to see because of the wind-driven intensity of the storm, I set about learning how to operate my new chain saw. I came within inches of cutting off my right leg the first time I fired it up.

On the second or third day I found I could no longer open the doors to the upstairs bedrooms. Other doors in the house still worked, but only with difficulty. As I pondered what might be causing this, a wooden awning mounted over one of the east-facing windows came crashing down onto the deck.

It didn't take long—though longer than it should have, because another awning came down in the meantime—to figure out that they were giving way under the weight of the snow. I cleared off the rest of the awnings before they met a similar fate, remembering as I did so a news report about whole houses caving in after an unusually heavy snowfall in New England.

A look up at the ceiling revealed that it was visibly sagging. That explained why the doors wouldn't open. It also meant I was going to have to do something—and quickly—about the several feet of snow sitting on our roof.

The roof was high and steep, especially on the north side, where the snow was deepest. I'd been up there once before, in warm, dry weather, and found it unnerving. But unless I was willing to take a chance on being buried alive under a collapsing house, I was going to have to climb up there again, this time in a blizzard.

A single misstep could be fatal. Even if I kept my footing, the wind was strong enough that a sudden gust could knock me off balance and send me tumbling to the ground. But once I'd cleared a patch large enough that I could stand on shingles rather than snowdrifts, I felt more secure. From then on it was mostly just hard physical labor.

It did the trick. The roof regained its normal shape, the doors worked again, and there was an added, completely unexpected side effect.

I haven't mentioned our dog yet, because, frankly, she'd been something of a disappointment. We'd rescued her from the San Francisco pound the day before setting off for Spy Rock, thinking we'd need a watchdog, and in observance of the principle that two stooges are generally in want of a third.

She was affectionate and cuddly, but the worst watchdog ever. If you made a sudden move or noise in her vicinity, she'd wet herself. But her biggest single liability was the fact that she either couldn't or wouldn't bark.

Before ending up at the pound, she'd lived in a tiny San Francisco apartment where, we guessed, she must have been beaten every time she made a noise. She was as nervous as the proverbial cat in a roomful of rocking chairs, and no matter how I tried, I couldn't coax so much as a growl or a whimper out of her.

I'd even tried to show her how it was done by crawling around the house on all fours, doing my best imitation of a barking dog. But while regarding me with some curiosity and concern, she showed no sign of wanting to join in. I'd reluctantly concluded that we'd have to trade her in for a fiercer model, or, since we'd already grown attached to her, get a second dog.

But everything changed that day as I shoveled off the roof. For reasons I may never understand unless I someday wind up being reincarnated as a dog, she was driven into a frenzy by the clumps of snow that I pushed over the side. Barking wildly, she chased down each and every one. Not a single shovelful of snow was allowed to fall to earth unbarked at.

Before that day, unable to agree on what to call her, we'd referred to her simply as "the dog." But now she'd earned her name—Ruf-Ruf. A bit foofy for a ferocious watchdog, perhaps, but you had to work with what you had—in her case, a cute but runty blond lab mix.

It wasn't a minute too soon for Ruf-Ruf to redeem herself, either. She'd been in the metaphorical doghouse (the actual one being buried outside under several feet of snow) since the first night of the storm.

That had been when we'd heard the pathetic cries of a tiny kitten crawling through the snow outside our front door. She couldn't have been more than five or six weeks old; where she'd come from and how she'd found her way to us remained a complete mystery.

We brought her in and tried to nurse her back to health by feeding her warm milk with an eyedropper. Most of the milk fell on the floor; she was too weak even to hold her head up, let alone swallow. But eventually, Mew-Mew (there'd been a kitten by this name in my first grade reader who I'd never quite forgotten) began to perk up.

She managed to get to her feet and take a few tentative steps across the kitchen floor. Ruf-Ruf, who'd been sitting there keeping an eye on the proceedings, gave a quick snap and with one bite broke little Mew-Mew's back. She died a few minutes later, with Ruf-Ruf lying on the floor giving us a plaintive look that seemed to say, "Now that that annoying creature is out of the way, how about playing with me?"

Things settled into a more comfortable routine by the fourth or fifth day of the storm. I was getting better with the chain saw, even learning which kinds of wood would burn best in our stove. The snow kept falling, but no longer seemed to be getting any deeper.

From time to time the skies would clear up briefly, allowing us to see down into the valley, where everything remained green and spring-like. Did anyone even know we were up here? The blizzard was the all-encompassing fact of our lives, but to judge from the news and the weather reports on the radio, which spoke cheerily about warm, sunny weather settling in over the flatlands, it had never even happened.

On the seventh day a hard freeze left the surface of the snow solid enough to walk on. It was like being let out of prison. I no longer had to dig my way around; now I could venture all over the land in search of wood. I walked down to the road, hoping to retrieve some things from the car, only to find it had vanished beneath the snow. After a few minutes of digging, my shovel hit metal and I discovered I'd been standing on its roof.

During the second week, life grew still easier, to the point where it began to feel like an extended holiday. We were getting several hours of sunshine every morning, though by afternoon the clouds would pile up again and enough snow would fall to replace any that might have melted. I'd accumulated a decent supply of firewood, so the house was warm and comfortable. Our main concern now was how long the food would hold out.

Early in the morning of Day Ten, we woke to a tremendous racket outside. Ruf-Ruf was barking her head off, but we could also hear human voices, the first voices other than our own that we'd heard since the storm began.

Frank, our neighbor from down the road, along with his brother-in-law and a couple other people from the Lower Loop, had come up the hill on skis and stopped to see if we were still alive. They'd run out of food, and were trying to make it into town.

Thanks to the CB radios that they, like many mountain people, used in lieu of telephones, they were able to bring us some news from the other side of the mountain. Drifts up on the ridge were said to be over ten feet deep, and a Caterpillar D4, the bulldozer normally used to build and grade our roads, had gotten hopelessly stuck trying to break through.

But Frank reckoned getting out on skis wouldn't be a problem, and asked if Anne and I were interested in coming along. We only had one pair of skis—Udo had left them behind when he moved out—and I knew they were of no use to me. I'd never skied in my life, and had unceremoniously fallen on my behind the one time I'd tried them on.

Anne was an experienced skier, however, and since she had business to attend to in the city anyway, it made sense for her to go. With only one mouth to feed, our food supply was more likely to outlast the storm, so off she went, while I stayed put and waited for the roads to clear.

It would be another two and a half weeks before that happened. "What did you do by yourself all that time?" people often asked. Not a lot, I'd tell them. And yet my days were strangely full. I played piano and guitar, read more than I had in years, listened obsessively to the radio, and spent an inordinate amount of time staring meaningfully out one window or another.

By mid-April the sun was high enough in the sky to bring some serious firepower to bear on the still abundant snowdrifts, and on south-facing slopes, patches of green began to emerge. In the daytime, at least, it was warm enough to believe that spring had finally returned.

But I only needed to round the bend at the top of my driveway to be transported back to midwinter. In the perpetual shade of the fir-lined north slopes, the road was still blocked by drifts as tall as I was.

Finally there came a week of unbroken sunshine, when even the nights stayed warm enough to do without a fire. Snow washed away in torrential streams, sometimes taking hillsides and roads with it. The flowers that had survived came back into bloom, and the hyacinths I'd planted beneath the windows filled the house with a heady perfume of possibility and promise.

I took long, meandering walks, venturing ever farther from my land until one day I realized that if I could get this far on foot, chances were good that the car would make it as well. And so it did; on the first of May I drove out, almost effortlessly, apart from a little slipping and sliding on the ridge top, where drifts still stood waist-high in spots alongside the road.

Once I'd dropped below the snow line, I saw that cars were already kicking up dust trails. The emerald green fields, dazzlingly bedecked with wild flowers, seemed to herald a languorous interval of respite and peace, but it was not to be. Spring fluttered by in the blink of an eye and the long hard summer began.

three

three

I might be exaggerating a little. We actually enjoyed a couple weeks of spring before summer hit with full superheated force. And there were at least a couple days of sub-freezing weather, which, I'd discover, could and probably would put in at least a token appearance any time up until late May. By the time I'd spent a few years on Iron Peak, I'd seen snow fall in every month but July.

Life in the mountains, I was to learn, is all about the elements. Everything ultimately comes down to some version of earth, air, fire, and water, with the latter two being the most critical.

In winter, fire is your friend; water, whether frozen or liquid, your enemy. In summer, things are turned around: in the tinder-dry hills a single spark can turn into a conflagration capable of wiping out in an afternoon what took years or decades to build. At that point, maintaining an adequate supply of water becomes an all-consuming quest.

Whether as snow or rain, between 50 and 100 inches of precipitation landed on Iron Peak annually. Between October and April, when nearly all of it fell, it was hard to imagine how a water shortage could ever be a problem. After months of over-flowing creeks and washed out roads, after being cut off from the world for weeks at a time by mountains of snow, it was tempting, once the sun came out, to sit back and watch the flowers grow.

Water was everywhere—no longer the muddy, raging torrents of winter, but fresh, clear, life-giving water. You could hear it crashing over the rocks down below, see it oozing out of the ground and collecting into rivulets that tracked the contours of every hillside.

Our storage tank stayed full to overflowing, thanks to the hydraulic ram pump Udo had installed in the creek. A ram pump uses the power produced by water as it tumbles downhill. Entering an intake pipe about 100 feet long, the water gathers momentum until it strikes a valve at the bottom end with enough force to trap a small amount on the uphill side of the valve. Each time the process is repeated—approximately every three to five seconds—more water is pushed upwards into a pipe that eventually empties into a tank on a hill above the house.

This technology had been around for millennia—Udo told me it had been invented by the ancient Romans—and was easy and economical to install. I wondered why more people didn't use it, then realized it was probably because they'd never heard of it, just as I hadn't before coming to the mountain. The pump could be assembled from parts available at any plumbing supply store, worked tirelessly night and day, and provided more water than we could use.

Until, that is, summer set in and the creek began to dry up. The ram didn't need much water to keep working; a pool five or six inches deep was plenty, as long as the mouth of the intake pipe remained submerged.

But if the water level dropped low enough to allow air into the line even momentarily, the ram would come to a juddering halt. The reassuring, rhythmic click and clack, that on quiet evenings I could hear echoing like a heartbeat across the land, went silent, as did the trickle and splash of water dropping gently into our tank.

Discouraging as that could feel, it was no big deal in itself. I could usually restart the pump by hand in a matter of seconds.

The 20 to 25 minutes it took to hike down to the creek and back up again were a bit more of a problem.

When Udo first showed me how the ram worked, he made a crack about how the two of us would still be clambering up and down that hillside when we were 80 years old. I thought that sounded kind of cool, but after the first few hundred times I made the journey, the idea lost some of its appeal.

Sometimes, though, when the weather wasn't too hot and I wasn't in a hurry, it was kind of fun. Like playing in the woods when I was a boy: forging trails, jumping over rocks and stumps, sliding on my backside when the hill got too steep to keep my balance. As a child I'd also loved splashing around in the water, something I would have countless opportunities to do that summer.

The creek bed was lined with stones of all shapes, sizes, and colors, ranging from pebbles to boulders, nearly all of which, at one time or another, wound up helping or hindering the ongoing engineering project that was my ram-powered water supply.

When winter rains turned the placid stream into a seething whitewater cauldron, rocks weighing more than I did would be tossed about like billiard balls, sometimes burying or even shattering the pipes and pump. I had to do a major rebuild job following the blizzard, thanks to the torrential runoff produced by the melting snow.

Once hot weather arrived, however, I could see the creek's water level inexorably dropping from one day to the next. My struggle then became one of maintaining a deep enough reservoir to supply the ram's intake pipe. I'd dig down into the creek until I hit bedrock, then build a dam to keep the water where it was needed. I'd use the rocks and dirt I'd dug up to construct a wall roughly two feet high and a foot thick.

But rocks and dirt alone didn't come close to being watertight enough to create a useful dam. Luckily, Udo had introduced me to a semi-miraculous substance, a bluish-colored clay that could be found in pockets all along the creek, most commonly at the base of the large blue rocks that had given the creek its semi-official name.

When wet, it was as malleable as the clay I'd played with as a child, and I'd use it like mortar to line the spaces between the rocks that made up my dam. As it dried, it would harden and turn light gray, until it could barely be distinguished from the rocks it bound together. Wet or dry, it did an astonishing job of sealing the dam; long after most of the creek had been reduced to a few desultory eddies and puddles, the ram had a foot-deep pool of crystal clear water to draw on.

But by mid-July my most herculean efforts could no longer provide enough water to keep the ram going. The time had come, as Udo had warned it would, to switch over to the electric pump he'd installed as a backup. An electric pump had advantages—it could deliver more water in an afternoon than the ram could in a day or two—but a whole new set of issues came with it. Unlike the ram, for example, which would harmlessly stop if it ran out of water, the electric pump would overheat and destroy itself within minutes of going dry.

Then there was the problem of electricity. Our house was powered mainly by solar panels, but we had a cranky, semi-reliable generator we could use as a backup battery charger or for running heavy machinery. I strung a couple hundred feet of wire through the woods and down the hill to connect the generator to the pump, but getting water was seldom as simple as turning it on and flipping a switch.

First there had to be at least one trip down to the creek to ensure there was sufficient water in the reservoir and, if necessary, to prime the pump. If all was in order, I could shout up to Anne to start the generator, but once it was running, she'd no longer be able to hear me, so any further communication required a trip back up the hill.

And as often as not, further communication would be essential: either the electricity wasn't coming through, or the pump had lost its prime, or a part had broken that could only be replaced via a trip to town. On a good day I'd be up and down the hill two or three times—on a not so good day, five or ten. And every few weeks there'd be a day when, despite climbing back and forth from dawn to dark, nothing would work and I'd fall into bed with not so much as a drop of water to show for my labors.

Plumbing-wise, we enjoyed a nicer setup than many mountain houses. Not only did we have an indoor toilet, but also a shower and bathtub, a kitchen sink, and outdoor hookups for watering the gardens. If you didn't know the water was coming from a tank located a couple dozen yards up the hill, it wouldn't have seemed that different from living in the city, where limitless amounts of water could be had at the turn of a tap.

But the 1,200 gallons our tank contained wouldn't last long in the heat of a Spy Rock summer. It seldom got as warm as it did down in town, where 100-degree days were typical, but my old-fashioned round metal thermometer advertising a local butcher ("Meats With Your Approval") routinely registered in the upper 80s and low 90s. And that was in the shade.

Out in the sun, it was another story: the fields where everything had been growing with science fiction-like rapidity—I sometimes dreamed that grasping tendrils of runaway vegetation had enveloped the house and were pushing their way in through the windows—went from green to yellow, and from yellow to brown. Muddy earth hardened into clay, which in turn dissolved into desiccated clumps that crumbled into dust underfoot.

There was only one thing that could keep this withering process at bay: water, and lots of it. That first summer we had a decent-sized vegetable garden, hundreds of flowers, a couple dozen fruit trees, and the fir and pine seedlings I'd planted out on the north face.

The seedlings were too widely spaced to water by hand, which was why most of them didn't make it, but nearly all the fruit trees survived, as did our tomatoes, zucchini, yellow squash, carrots, corn, peas, and cucumbers. And then there were Anne's half dozen marijuana plants, tucked away in a semi-shady corner below the house.

To keep all this going, as well as to provide for our personal needs, five or six hundred gallons of water a day would have been ideal, but drip irrigation and careful conservation helped keep our use down to a little more than half that. Even still, our tank could never hold much of a cushion. If the pump was out of commission for more than a couple days, or the tank sprang a leak, the little oasis we'd carved out of the arid hillside would vanish more quickly than it had appeared.

Luckily, it never happened, although there were some close calls. The worst was when a part on the pump motor shattered (almost taking my eye with it) and we had to wait through the weekend for a replacement. But by late August, after living in what had felt like crisis mode for months, I almost began to feel like I could relax once in a while.

Although things, even potentially disastrous things, still went wrong, they no longer bothered me as much. I had learned that no matter how bleak matters looked, there was usually help of some kind at hand. Udo knew how to handle most plumbing and electrical problems, and I'd gotten to know several other neighbors I could call on in emergencies.

I was lucky, too, that Anne was more adept at mechanical and carpentry issues than I was. She had an uncanny talent for improvising solutions out of spare parts and scraps. She'd also done wonders with the house, making curtains, hanging pictures and handmade decorations, and scouring every thrift shop on the North Coast for furniture, dishes, and the various accoutrements of country life.

What little decorating and improvement I did mostly took place outdoors. I became a compulsive flower planter, not just around the house, but almost anywhere I thought something had a chance of growing. I also bought a couple dozen sets of wind chimes and a box of four hundred crystal prisms from some hippie supply store, and hung them in trees all across the property.

The mountain winds were hard on the chimes—only a handful of them lasted more than a year or two—but the crystals would endure for decades. I could be walking almost anywhere on the land and suddenly find my eyes stabbed by dazzling blasts of pure colored light. People laughed at me for spending hard-earned money decorating the forest, but the way I saw it, the tinkling bells and unpredictable flashing rainbows helped transform a beautiful place into a magical one.

Life also became less stressful when I began to adapt to what people referred to as "mountain time." Its basic principles were that a) everything took at least twice as long as it should; and b) anything or anybody you were waiting for might show up an hour, a day, or a week late. If at all.

It could be annoying and frustrating if you weren't used to it, but mountain time had its charming aspects, too. You might be clearing brush down by the road and wave to a passing neighbor. He in turn would probably stop for a freewheeling chat that could last the rest of the morning and into the afternoon.

Or he might enlist you to help pull somebody's car out of a ditch, which would end up turning into a dinner invitation and a night spent strumming guitars and swapping stories at a house you'd never seen before and couldn't find again if you had to. That brush wouldn't clear itself, true, but it'd be patiently waiting for you when, or if, you showed up again the following morning.

Our nearest neighbors were Frank and Linda, who lived about a mile downhill, and Jim and Jenny, whose A-frame of logs and corrugated steel sat a similar distance up the road. With long, braided hair, Jim bore a more than passing resemblance to Willie Nelson, and dressed almost exclusively in a buckskin suit he'd made from a traditional Native American pattern. At the drop of a coonskin cap (yes, he had one of those, too), he'd have his guitar out and be plinking away at "Blue Eyes Crying In The Rain."

Jim and Jenny had two daughters, Bex and Sarah. Frank's wife, Linda, was Jenny's sister, and also had two kids, Lori and Frank. To avoid confusion, the younger Frank (officially Frank lll), went by the name of Tre.

Before coming to the mountains, Big Frank had been a helicopter pilot in Vietnam. On being discharged from the military, he'd wanted to get as far as possible from the traumatic sights and sounds he'd experienced there. Spy Rock must have seemed like just the ticket when he discovered it. Little did he—or any of us, really—know what lay ahead.

Anne and I had already met all these folks in passing, but started getting to know them better the afternoon we trekked down to the local swimming hole known as Snake Lake. This little pond got its name from the bright green water snakes that swarmed around you and went streaking between your legs as soon as you entered the water. They took a little getting used to, but the snakes weren't going to keep anybody from diving in on those hot summer days—not even the dogs, who splashed and swam as happily as their owners.

On that particular afternoon, most of the women and children from our neck of the woods were there, along with Udo's wife Josie and her kids, Kain and Kira. I marveled at the way mountain kids seemed better behaved and more mature than their counterparts in the city, more at ease with adults, and, at the same time, more carefree and playful. Kids, in other words, who weren't embarrassed about being kids.

It would take time, but that day felt like the beginning of our acceptance into Spy Rock society. Once people became more at ease with Anne and me, it became clear that their first impressions of us hadn't necessarily been good ones. That shouldn't have been surprising; even in San Francisco we were often considered weirdos. Our short hair, punky/new wave fashions, and failure to conform to conventional gender roles raised eyebrows and set tongues wagging all around the mountain.

Newcomers were almost by default suspected of being narcs, at least until they'd demonstrated otherwise, and we were no exception. The fact that we stuck out like sore thumbs, and that real narcs would be more successful if they came cloaked in the garb of longhaired, bearded Deadheads, didn't seem to matter.

Once Anne let it be known that she had her own marijuana garden, people opened up, offering suggestions about how to camouflage it and increase her yield. At the same time, they wondered aloud why she'd put in so few plants, and why, since marijuana growing was generally seen as men's work, I hadn't put in any at all.

My frequently repeated declarations that I didn't want to grow dope, and that Anne's patch was just a hobby garden, made us all the stranger by Spy Rock standards. Even still, we began getting invited to mountain parties, which were surprisingly wholesome affairs, not unlike a cross between the barn-raisings of pioneer times (on one occasion we actually did pitch in to lift and affix a new wall to somebody's house) and old-fashioned church socials.

Kids would tear through the woods or swing from ropes hanging in the trees, while the men shuffled their feet in the dust and muttered laconically about engine troubles or the latest rumors of marijuana busts. The ladies talked about each other's relationships and bemoaned the absence of any decent culture or shopping north of Santa Rosa.

Someone would start playing music, a target would be set up for an axe or knife throwing competition, and festivities would roll on into the night, with the children falling asleep in quiet corners or the back seats of cars. Around about midnight, someone would start a general exodus, declaring, "Hoo boy, time I should be going, I've got to be up at the crack of dawn to patch that leaky old pump line." Twenty minutes later all would be silent again, as if the songs and laughter and voices had been no more than a fleeting illusion.

When I say "silent," I'm talking, of course, about human sounds. Nights, especially summer nights, produced such a raucous symphony of crickets and owls and mysterious rustles and crackling twigs that it's a wonder anyone got any sleep at all. The only time you'd guess people inhabited those hills was when the whine and rumble of someone's truck making a late night return from town came echoing down the canyon.

As summer starts winding to a close, tension ratchets up around the various homesteads. There's the perennial question of whether the water will hold out until the rains come, the race to get enough firewood cut and seasoned, and the dilemma of what do with the tomatoes and zucchini and cucumbers that in those last golden days seem to ripen faster than you can pick them.

Above all, there's the nervousness, the edginess, sometimes the sheer terror, centered around how well—or if—the marijuana harvest will come in. A stranger spotted on the road can send waves of paranoia rippling through the community. Does he belong to a gang of thieves scoping out their next ripoff? Could he be the advance guard of a police raid that might not only seize the year's crop, but also haul Dad and Mom off to jail and the kids into Child Protective Services?

Nowadays, when every grower astute enough to fill out the appropriate paperwork has reinvented himself or herself as a "medical marijuana provider," the threat of prison has mostly receded, but at that time it was still a real concern. Even then, though, prison sentences were beginning to happen less frequently, not least because there were simply more growers than the authorities could hope to catch, let alone find room for in the County Jail. By the summer of 1982, it was beginning to look like the cops might have given up altogether.

There would be moments of panic when a low-flying plane or helicopter circled overhead, but actual raids were few and far between. From worrying about whether they'd make it through the harvest unscathed, growers switched to complaining that they'd have put in twice as many plants if they'd known law enforcement was going to give them such an easy time this year.

I even caught myself wishing I'd done a little growing. It wasn't that I'd gone back on my resolution to stay out of the marijuana business, but I could have used the money. Country living was turning out to be more expensive than I'd expected.

By September the blisters on my hands had hardened into calluses from splitting what looked like enough firewood to see us through the winter. I had acquired new muscles, new survival skills, and a slowly growing confidence that yes, maybe I could make it up here on Iron Peak.

I still managed to set off a chimney fire the first time I used the stove that fall, but spent only a couple minutes panicking before remembering how to put it out. And when the solar electric system went haywire, I was able to fix it myself without running to Udo for help. But satisfaction with my accomplishments was tempered by the awareness that I was constantly playing catch-up.

Weeds grew, pipes leaked, pumps broke faster than I could pull, patch, or repair them. In the spring, I'd noticed black raspberry bushes growing wild everywhere, and watched their progress through May and June, looking forward to a glorious harvest. We'd have berries with ice cream, I thought, bake them into pies, put up enormous jars of jam to last us through the winter.

The raspberries started ripening around the Fourth of July. I picked a handful and ate them as I was working around the yard, but before I thought to head out with a bucket to collect more, they were gone, either gobbled up by animals or shriveled by the hot sun.

Similarly, one of my newly planted trees unexpectedly produced a couple dozen cherries. I never tasted any; the birds, who'd kept a sharper eye on them than I had, and who got up a lot earlier, nabbed every single one. That symbolized the summer for me: long on promise, short on delivery, except when it came to sweat, dust, and backbreaking work.

But we'd survived, confounding not only my own expectations, but also those of the neighbors, who, I learned, had all but been taking bets on how long the punk rock city slickers would last. Anne's marijuana crop came in, not in huge quantities, but with more than enough to keep her happy. The hillsides and forests turned multiple shades of red, gold, and purple, and October delivered a series of deliciously warm days during which the land seemed to stretch languorously under the last rays of a fast fading sun.

Once the month was finished, cold winds swept in from the northeast, and the distant peaks of the Yolla Bollys acquired their first coating of snow. November's snows didn't last long on our own mountains, but December's did; by Christmas the roads were covered with a thick layer of ice.

I'd traded in my ridiculous Honda for a 4WD Subaru. The new car tore effortlessly through ordinary snow, but without tire chains, didn't deliver enough traction to keep me from getting stranded one hair-raising afternoon on a patch of ice just inches away from a cliff.

Whether I tried to go forward, backward, uphill or downhill, the second I released the handbrake I would start sliding sideways toward oblivion. Half an hour of this left me on the verge of a nervous breakdown, but shoveling some rocks and sand under the wheels finally enabled me to make my escape. If only just.

Something similar happened to my dad on Christmas morning. Driving up from the city with my mother and my two brothers, he found himself hopelessly stuck at the bottom of a hill that his tires just couldn't get a grip on. Thankfully some neighbors came to his rescue, but he was still fuming when he walked in the door, letting me know what he thought about people who chose to live "on some mountain in the middle of nowhere."

Apart from that discordant note, our first Christmas on Iron Peak was almost picture perfect. For the first time in years, the whole family was together, including my sister and her two kids (with another on the way), who, along with my ne'er-do-well brother-in-common-law, had finally moved into their place on the other side of the mountain.

I lopped off the top ten feet of a Doug fir and dragged it up the hill to serve as our Christmas tree. With the winter sun spending most of its time behind clouds, trees, and ridge tops, our solar system could hardly keep up with the demands of the lights we strung it with, but we lit them anyway, casting a multicolored glow up and down the mountainside.

We added two more leaves to the table, stretching it out to accommodate the extended family. Feasting and celebration went on late into the night. Apart from the year I turned four, when Santa Claus brought me that American Flyer train set, it was the happiest Christmas I'd ever known.

Outside, new snow was falling gently and the woods were silent and still, dark yet luminous. There would be more struggles, more trials and, no doubt, more failures. But in that moment, I knew I was exactly where I needed and wanted to be, that nowhere else in the world could feel so right. Against all odds, we'd come to this wilderness and made it our home.

four

four

"As soon as you give a name to something, it begins to die," says an old Chinese proverb. Its corollary might be, "As soon as you get comfortable somewhere, things start to go wrong."

That had always been my experience, anyway. I thought, or at least hoped, it might be different on Spy Rock. For a while it was. Trouble might have been brewing down the road, but I saw—or maybe chose to see—no sign of it, and life settled into a pleasant, easy routine.

December's ice and snow were washed away by an early January rainstorm, and after that our second winter was like a dream compared with our first. At one point it rained every day for a month, but temperatures stayed relatively warm. My biggest challenge, thanks to all the rain—the back porch gauge recorded 120 inches that winter—was keeping our road from washing down the hill.

That job required many long hours with a pick and shovel, clearing rocks and mud from drainage ditches and culverts. It wasn't hard work, just time-consuming. Decked out in rubber boots, rain suit, and hat, I felt all but impervious to the elements, almost like a deep-sea diver or an astronaut.

I played engineer, as I'd done in the creek the summer before, digging channels to guide the runoff where it needed to go, letting the water itself do most of the heavy lifting. When flowing freely, it would carry off rocks and dirt faster than I could shovel them.

With the soil loosened to an almost soup-like consistency

by the constant rainfall, dozens of trees came down. Some were considerate enough to fall near or on the road, which made cutting and transporting firewood back to the house far easier than it had been the previous year. When 1 wasn't repairing culverts or hauling wood, I'd take the truck out in search of distinctively colored and shaped rocks, which 1 used to build borders around the house and gardens.

Before coming to the mountain 1 hadn't been a big fan of the outdoors, and was all but allergic to physical labor. But this was a new me, and 1 was enjoying the heck out of it. Anne and 1 were getting along better than ever, and apart from the occasional crisis—the wood stove backing up in a windstorm, a leaking or broken water pipe, a balky generator—life ticked along nicely.

One of the best things about that year on Spy Rock was getting to know my sister's kids, Jethro and Gabrielle. They were nine and seven years old, but because they'd been living either in England, where they were born, or Michigan, where my sister brought them after her marriage broke up, I'd never had the chance to spend any significant time with them.

The children often came to stay with us for a day or two, especially when my sister was in the latter stages of her pregnancy. Watching Anne pushing them around the yard in a wheelbarrow or helping them with their homework brought me closer than I'd ever come to thinking it might be time we started a family of our own.

Anne and 1 talked about it, and it felt like we were more or less in agreement that one day we'd be getting married and having children, but something—to this day 1 have no idea what—held us back from making it official. 1 liked to think we were en route to living happily ever after, but doing it on mountain time.

Another thing that seemed to be proceeding on mountain time was our quest to find a bassist for the band we'd been trying to start almost since we met in 1981. We'd tried out a couple people while still living in the Bay Area, but that had gone nowhere. Now, on Spy Rock, where punk rock was an alien, almost unheard of concept, it seemed ludicrous to hope we'd find someone willing to play with us.

The mountain was awash in musicians, but with few exceptions they fell somewhere along the Grateful Dead-reggae-endless boogie continuum. They'd listen uncomplainingly, and sometimes even join in, when I offered up my acoustic guitar renditions of old Hank Williams and Bob Dylan standards, but punk rock? Not interested. Not even slightly.

Things began looking more hopeful when our friend Richard moved up from the Bay Area to re-occupy land his grandfather had farmed along the Eel River earlier in the century. Situated several miles beyond where Spy Rock Road petered out into near-wilderness, the property had sat vacant since the Northwestern Pacific Railroad, which provided the only access, shut down passenger service in the late 1950s.

In defiance of what most reasonable people would think possible, Richard made his way to and from the old homestead through an incredibly demanding combination of walking, climbing, and mountain biking. Somehow he still found time and energy to travel over to our house for practice sessions with our as yet unnamed band. Though relatively new to the bass, he was no slouch, and at last it looked like we were getting somewhere.

Somewhere, maybe, but not yet where we wanted, which was playing gigs, making records, and having an impact on a Northern California punk scene that at the time felt like it was fading away. Looked at realistically, our lack of success shouldn't have been surprising; we were, after all, in the middle of nowhere, with the nearest venues for our kind of music located a hundred miles north in Arcata and almost two hundred miles south in San Francisco.

Making matters worse, while Anne and I had been making music together—trying to, anyway—for over two years, it wasn't, as they say, gelling. The sad truth was that we spent more time arguing than playing.

It couldn't have been fun for Richard, who, after his arduous trip up and over the mountain, had to stand around awkwardly while Anne and I debated, well, everything. The arguments weren't about song structure or arrangements, though they might have seemed to be; the real issue was that she and I kept plowing away at our instruments in our own directions, oblivious to, or even angered by, what the other was playing.

She was a good, powerful drummer and I was, shall we say, improving on the guitar, but we were working at cross-purposes. Smashing and bashing our way through the summer of 1983, we made little progress toward becoming a real band. It was a disappointment but not a surprise when Richard announced he was giving up on the project and moving back to the Bay Area.

Meanwhile, bigger trouble was afoot. Since there'd been almost no raids the previous summer, marijuana growers were cautiously optimistic about the future, believing they might at last be left to ply their trade in peace. But there were rumors about a new strike force, one in which federal and state authorities would join local law enforcement to launch an unprecedented crackdown on the devil weed.

There were always rumors on the mountain, of course. Sometimes it felt like paranoia was the common currency binding us all together. A favorite story that season had the Army using helicopters to spray our hillsides with Paraquat, or even Agent Orange, to wipe out marijuana farming once and for all.

That chemical assault never materialized, but the helicopters did: huge, thumping beasts, some of them giant Hueys left over from Vietnam, striking fear into the hearts of anyone in their path. My first encounter with one came as I meandered up to the crest of the hill overlooking the canyon carved out by Iron Creek. I heard the deep rumble of a helicopter's engine, felt the ground vibrating with the thwack-thwack of its rotors, but couldn't for the life of me figure out where the sound was coming from.

Until, that is, the Huey burst up out of the canyon to confront me at more or less eye level. Rising a bit higher, it hovered above the old oak tree at the top of the driveway while soldiers—National Guardsmen or Army Reserves in full battle regalia, automatic rifles dangling at the ready—hung from its sides, giving me the several times over.

We didn't have much to hide—Anne's dozen spindly plants were in the woods below the house, all but invisible from the air—but I was frightened nonetheless. This went beyond any police action I'd ever witnessed; it felt like war. And in a crucial sense, it was: although there was no shooting, no napalm, little physical violence to speak of, the Campaign Against Marijuana Planting—CAMP, as it would become known—seemed designed to wipe out an entire way of life.

It's hard to overstate how important marijuana was to the local economy and culture. While it wouldn't be fair to say that people lived in the mountains only to grow dope, few of them would have been able to live there if it weren't for dope. Local law enforcement efforts had been completely unable to keep up with the escalating size and scope of the marijuana trade; as a result, the crops got larger, more money flooded into the community, and people became more comfortable. Too comfortable, as it turned out.

The new 4x4s and satellite TV dishes that made sense a year or two earlier no longer looked like such a bright idea once CAMP appeared on the scene. Where in the past a grower might have had a 90% chance of bringing his crop to harvest, it was now more like a 50/50 proposition. And that was only if you lived in an area that CAMP wasn't specifically targeting.

Our land was bordered on three sides by empty parcels where nobody lived or grew, and our neighbors who did grow kept it fairly low key, so the helicopters didn't linger too long in our immediate vicinity. A couple miles down the road, it was a different story: day after day, the copters would appear at dawn, systematically moving from one piece of property to the next until everyone was wiped out.

Those of us who weren't raided still had to contend with the stress. To be awakened by the deafening, dish-rattling roar of a helicopter hovering directly overhead, or to listen to the insistent whine of a low-flying plane as it makes a dozen passes up and down your hillside, can fall somewhere between nerve-wracking and terrifying even if you don't have anything, or in our case, very much, to hide.

When winter finally settled in that year, it was over a shell-shocked mountain. People, especially those with kids, talked about giving up on this whole back-to-the-land thing. Some had already moved into town, and would henceforth use their mountain property only for growing. The community I'd finally begun to feel part of looked like it might be falling apart.

It was often the women who were most anxious to move off the mountain, but some of the kids, too, especially the teenagers, were itching for the bright lights of Willits or Ukiah. Laytonville had a perfectly adequate high school—at least for a town of barely a thousand people—but not much action. The only reason they didn't roll up the sidewalks at night was that, for the most part, there weren't any.

At every party, social gathering, or roadside chat, the talk was of whether to stay or go. There was endless speculation about the future of the mountain if the CAMP onslaught continued, and the most common refrain heard that winter was, "I'm not putting up with another year like this one."

Anne and I had come through all right—at least we hadn't been raided—but her tiny garden hadn't brought in much in the way of money. And my own income had dropped dramatically since we'd come to Spy Rock. I'd had enough savings to tide us over for a while, so I coasted along on the assumption that I'd figure something out when it became necessary.

There'd been a lot of coasting and not much figuring by the time 1984 rolled around, but I still wasn't prepared to admit how serious my predicament was. You'd think I would have at least confided in Anne about our money problems, but of course I didn't. Long after I could no longer afford to, I went on trying to pretend everything was fine.

Instead of leveling with her, I'd hint that we should economize a bit, that we didn't really need that piece of furniture or weekend in San Francisco she'd had her heart set on. Subtlety not being one of my strong points, I'd come across as heavy-handed and mean-spirited. We'd argue, harsh words would be exchanged, and eventually I'd try to patch things up by buying her something more expensive than what she'd asked for in the first place.

What she wanted most, and had been talking about as long as we'd been together, was a trip to Europe. In more prosperous times, I'd promised we'd go someday, but for the first years on the mountain, the idea of getting away for that long felt impossible. There were too many things to be looked after, too many things that could go wrong.

But by the winter of 1983-84 I was running out of reasons to put off the trip (apart from the obvious one of telling her we couldn't afford it). The weather had been mild, we hadn't had to contend with too many blizzards, washed out roads, or downed trees, and neighbors agreed to feed the animals and keep an eye on the house.

So off we went for six tumultuous weeks, returning in time to find the lush green grass of early spring spreading its mantle over and around everything we'd built and planted for the past two years. It was a stunning sight, one that has remained fixed in my memory, the sort of vision that would keep Spy Rock forever rooted in my soul.

Anne and I did a bit of fighting as we made our way across Europe, but the trip helped alleviate some of the tension between us. It made our money situation that much worse, of course, and hastened the day of reckoning. As spring rolled on toward summer, we resumed sniping at each other, as often as not about meaningless things rather than what was really bothering us.

Despite that unpleasantness, it would be the most beautiful of all my Spy Rock springs, the most glorious, green, and enduring. Even in July the creek was still flowing and the hills were alive with fresh growth. The uneasiness and awkwardness undermining our relationship never went away completely, but did recede into the background for a while.

In April I brought home a new puppy. Anne hadn't exactly asked for another dog, but knowing how much she loved animals, I didn't see how I could go wrong when, on the spur of the moment, I picked up a little black mutt, one of a litter some hippies were giving away in front of Geiger's.

With Ruf-Ruf still falling short on the watchdog front—she could bark up a storm, but went running for cover in the face of anything that looked like real danger—I thought we needed a bigger, braver dog to help out. And with a new pet to dote over, Anne might be too distracted to notice some of my own failings.

I was partly right. She questioned the need for another dog, but took to the newcomer immediately. Because the puppy's face uncannily resembled that of a gorilla—which was why I'd guessed, mistakenly as it turned out, that he'd grow up to be a good watchdog—I named him Kong.

That same month we finally found a bass player for our band. He'd been right there under our noses all along: Udo's 13-year-old son, Kain. True, he didn't yet know how to play the bass, but I considered that a minor drawback. He was willing to learn, lived locally, and was at least moderately enthusiastic about being in a band with us.

First things first, though: before we started practicing, I had to give him his official punk rock name. Keeping with the ape theme, I decided he'd be known as Kain Kong. Unlike our new dog, he didn't have the face of a gorilla, but even at 13 he was showing signs of being built like one.

The CAMP raiders were back in full force that summer. They'd abandoned the oversized Hueys in favor of smaller, faster, quieter copters, making it easier for them to dip down into the canyons and sneak up on farmers. They were as likely to be seen hugging the hillsides below as roaming the skies overhead.

Considering what had happened to many of our neighbors the previous year, I was halfway hoping Anne wouldn't put in any plants, but I knew that wasn't realistic. If nothing else, we needed the money. This became all the more painfully clear as we inched our way through those last nail-biting weeks before the harvest.

I still couldn't bring myself to admit how dire our situation was, which created the potential for the simplest of shopping trips to degenerate into a battle of ill wills. In the past I'd just hand her whatever money she said she needed; now I quibbled and bickered over every penny.

Even when she did something that would ultimately prove helpful, like doubling the size of that year's marijuana garden, I criticized and complained, suggesting she was putting us both at risk so she could earn extra spending money for herself. In reality, we were unlikely to get busted; Anne had become a skillful grower, and part of that skill involved knowing how to effectively camouflage her plants.

This meant keeping them in the woods below the house, where a steeply declining and heavily forested hillside made it impossible for the helicopters to get close enough for a good look. Using that technique, you missed out on much of the sunlight, and as a result produced smaller yields, but that was how everybody had to operate now if they wanted to stay in business. You compensated by putting in more plants and spreading them over a wider area.

The scariest moments that summer came not from CAMP, but from a fast-moving forest fire that broke out in the Eel River canyon. Fires were not unusual in late summer, when thunderclouds would build up over the mountains and bombard them with dry lightning strikes. It was why the lookout tower atop Iron Peak was so vital.

But most of those fires erupted in higher, more remote locations, usually on the far side of the river. This time was different. The flames came charging up the hills directly below us, and for a few gut-wrenching days looked as though they might consume everything on our side of the mountain.

Faced with a situation like that, you have to decide—sometimes with little or no notice—whether to evacuate while it's still possible, or to stay, in hopes that even if the fire burns through your land, you'll be able to save your house.

Though I'd added an extra water tank, doubling our storage capacity, 2,400 gallons wouldn't go far toward staving off a forest fire. The sensible thing—and what the Forest Service constantly recommended—was to clear all vegetation away from the house for 50 to 100 feet. But I hadn't moved to the wilderness to live on a barren, sun-baked patch of rocks and clay, so our house remained closely surrounded on three sides by pleasant but potentially flammable groves of pine, fir and oak.

If a fire ever got close, it would leap from treetop to treetop and inevitably spill onto our roof, deck, and walls. The house would be a goner within minutes. I rationalized that in a worst-case scenario, I could grab the chain saw, strip away the most dangerous branches and brush, and then use the hose to keep the flames at bay.

This idea was sheer fantasy, of course. The kind of job I was envisioning would require a whole crew of men working for a day or two; when a fire shifted course and came at you, you might have five or ten minutes. I stood on my back deck, watching with morbid fascination as the copters circled Iron Peak to fill up with water from a pond on the north face, then returned to empty their loads on the advancing flames.

It seemed so ineffectual, like organizing a bucket brigade to cool off an erupting volcano, but there was nothing else to be done. The terrain was too steep and inaccessible, and the fire too massive, for there to be any hope of fighting it on the ground. At least the winds remained light to moderate, but what wind there was kept pushing the flames in our direction.

Finally the smoke grew so thick that breathing became difficult, so we packed up the dogs and retreated to the coast. Only 25 miles away as the crow flies, but nearly two hours by car, the beach near Fort Bragg was a world apart from the choking inferno we'd left behind.

We found the seashore wrapped in its usual summer clouds and fog, with the temperature struggling to make it into the 60s. Being able to breathe again was an incredible relief, but even here we could see great clouds of smoke billowing over the mountains to the east.

After we'd holed up in a motel for a couple days, the smoke died down, and we heard on the news that the fire had been brought under control. What we didn't hear, and what nobody seemed to know, was how much, if any, of Iron Peak had burned. The only way we were going to find out was to go home and see for ourselves. If, that is, we still had a home to go to.

As we rounded the last bend on the ridge top, right before the road dives down into the forest, I could hardly bear to look. From that point you can see all the way to the Eel River, and I would know in an instant if the fire had reached our land.

It hadn't. The firefighters had done a heroic job, and our side of the mountain had mostly been spared. A few sparse plumes of smoke drifted off to the south and east, but the forest was intact and no homes had been lost. Better still, CAMP hadn't been able to operate all week, bringing us that much closer to a safe harvest.

I was happy to find I still had a home, of course, but was almost equally pleased that relatively few trees had been lost. I was surprised, in fact, at how passionately I had come to care about the forest, almost as though it were a living thing with which I had a personal relationship.

It hadn't always been that way. On the day I met Anne, in May of 1981, she and I were walking in Marin County, past some redwood trees silhouetted against a pristine blue sky. I noticed her noticing me admiring the view, but instead of remarking, "Beautiful, isn't it?" as a normal person might, I snarled, "I hate nature." It was in that moment, Anne told me, that she'd decided I was a "real" punk, and perhaps began to fall in love with me.

I hadn't really hated nature, not that much, anyway. I just knew that expressing contempt for it was a surefire way to shock the bourgeoisie, especially in the sproutier sectors of the Bay Area. But now that I was living in a place where people and their works were barely noticeable and trees nearly as numerous as stars in the sky, my tune had changed.

I won't say I went around communing with the earth spirits, but I did spend a great deal of time wandering wide-eyed in the forest, observing how things fit together, how certain trees and plants flourished while others were crowded out. I also saw the ravages that remained from when the land had last been logged.

Decaying stumps of old growth trees that would have dwarfed anything still standing, denuded hillsides that had collapsed into the creek and filled it with rock and silt: it didn't make a pretty picture. The land was resilient and recovering, but it would be decades—perhaps centuries—before it would regain its former glory.

I made a promise—okay, maybe I did talk to trees now and then—that as long as I had any power to prevent it, no logger would ply his trade on this land again. Around that same time a minor hubbub erupted after somebody cut down a couple of the last remaining trees along Highway 101 in Laytonville. They weren't old growth—the term commonly used to describe trees that predated the white man's arrival in these hills—but they were nice tall Doug firs that lent a hint of shade and gentility to what was otherwise a sun-blasted asphalt and gravel desert.

The trees had been removed, it was claimed, to make room for a parking lot, but once the parking lot was built, it became clear that they hadn't been in the way at all. It looked like the only reason they'd been felled was to conform with someone's idea of neat and orderly parking lot management. Someone from Los Angeles, I suspected.

I wrote a letter to the *Laytonville Ledger* expounding this view. The *Ledger* was an eight-page weekly whose writing and layout compared—not always favorably—with that of my high school newspaper. But it had its good points, one being its letters to the editor pages. You might not find much news in the *Ledger*, but there were some rip-roaring arguments.

The reaction to my letter about the trees got far livelier than I had expected. I'd assumed all right-thinking citizens would agree with me; as it turned out, most of them barely noticed the trees were gone, but took great offense at my description of "downtown" Laytonville as an unattractive rural slum with few redeeming qualities.

I hadn't intended to insult Laytonville—though it might have been hard to tell from the language I used—as much as I'd wanted to bemoan the loss of one of those redeeming qualities. It didn't matter: the next week's issue of the *Ledger* contained a barrage of letters directed at me, mostly variations on "Love it or leave it," "If you don't like it, go back where you came from," and "Who does this Livermore guy think he is anyway?"

Who indeed? That letter would mark the debut of my Lawrence (later shortened to Larry) Livermore persona. I'd originally acquired it as a nickname while writing my 1979 novel, which centered around a nuclear disaster at the Bay Area's Lawrence Livermore National Laboratory. My birth name being Lawrence, my girlfriend at the time thought it would be hilarious to start referring to me as Lawrence D. Livermore.

Nothing came of the novel—it was never published, and was read only by a handful of long-suffering friends—so the joke had been all but forgotten until 1 started looking for a punk name to go with my band. But since the band hadn't done anything of note yet, signing my letter to the *Ledger* was the first time 1 publicly used the name that everyone but my parents would soon know me by.

1 was astounded at how quickly it caught on. Few people had known or cared what Larry Hayes thought about things, but the moment he turned into Lawrence Livermore, he became the talk of the town. Dismayed that the reaction to my letter hadn't been more positive, but delighted by all the attention 1 was getting, 1 parked myself in front of the typewriter and dashed off bitter screeds on everything from the lack of local composting facilities to the war in Nicaragua.

By October the *Ledger*'s editor had received so many complaints about me that he stopped printing my letters. 1 shifted my efforts farther afield, addressing diatribes to the *Willits News* and the *San Francisco Chronicle*. They'd occasionally print the ones dealing with national and international affairs, but had little interest in the tempests brewing up in Laytonville's tiny teapot.

So when it came to opinionating on local matters, I'd effectively been silenced. "The hell with the *Ledger*," 1 said angrily. "I'll start my own newspaper."

Anne greeted this announcement with one of her patented eye rolls, but 1 was serious. 1 banged out four typewritten pages that included a mission statement, a report on the year's marijuana harvest, and an account of a bear that had broken into a neighbor's house and helped itself to milk and cookies from an overturned refrigerator.

I took my work down to Spare Time Supply, a Willits nursery and feed store that had the only reliable xerox machine in the north county. Stacking and collating the finished pages atop bags of manure—a fitting beginning, local wags would point out for years to come—I ran off 50 copies of the *Iron Peak Lookout*.

Setting aside her initial doubts about this latest crusade of mine, Anne had helped me by drawing a logo that featured the pagoda-like fire tower whose windows, seen from a distance, resembled eyes keeping watch over our mountain. I gave a few copies to friends, left a dozen at the Post Office—the one spot in town where everyone eventually turned up—and distributed the rest at gathering places and stopping points in town and on the mountain.

At least half of them were defaced or destroyed immediately. I'd expected the more conservative townspeople to be unimpressed by my efforts, but was shocked to find the most virulent opposition to the *Iron Peak Lookout* coming from my neighbors on the mountain—the very people I thought I was creating it for.

Their main objection was that I was "drawing heat" onto Spy Rock by writing about marijuana, even though I'd made a point of talking about dope growing only in the most general terms. And, as I pointed out, the *San Francisco Chronicle* and a couple of TV stations had already done far more revealing features about our area.

Didn't matter. "If you want to keep living here," I was told, even by neighbors I considered friends, "you need to find a different hobby."

I refused to take their advice seriously. I was already busy composing issue #2, though it would be several months before it came out—partly because I was still dazed and confused by the fallout #1 had produced, but even more so because of some dramatic developments on the home front.

First came the arrival from London of my wonderful Aunt Olivia, who wasn't really my aunt—she was actually grandmother to Jethro and Gabrielle, my sister's two older kids—and wasn't really named Olivia—she'd adopted it because she found Olive, the name she was born with, "too boring and English."

She showed up just as my relationship with Anne was entering its final downward trajectory. Olivia's presence—and it was quite a presence; she was not exactly one for sitting quietly in the corner—may have postponed but could not avert the end. Anne and I were reluctant to fight in front of her, but we replaced verbal fireworks with sullen brooding and studious avoidance.

Our latest conflict—the one which would prove to be our last—revolved around Anne's eagerness, and my refusal, to spend part of the winter in Brazil. We had friends there, so places to stay would have been no problem, but, I told her, we couldn't afford the plane fare or the bars-and-restaurants Rio lifestyle.

Anne argued that her marijuana earnings would cover the cost. What she didn't know—and what I refused to tell her—was that her marijuana income might be the only income we'd have that year. With no way of knowing that the easy money of the early 80s was gone, possibly never to return, she assailed me as being stingy, cantankerous, and no fun at all.

It was true that I wasn't much fun, and hadn't been in a while. I worried constantly about money, couldn't stop ranting, raving, and fighting with the neighbors about one political cause or another, and was consumed with frustration over our band's lack of progress. Kain had turned out to be a great bassist, but as had been the case with Richard, all too often had to spend our practice sessions standing around watching Anne and me fight.

I also struggled with a general sense of depression, a feeling that my life had not turned out at all the way I thought it should. Increasingly I came to believe it would be a miracle if anyone wanted to stay with me. As much as I feared being left on my own, I knew in my heart it was only a matter of time before Anne would be gone. I may have known it before she did.

We spent New Year's Eve at the Howling Wolf Lodge, an unusual bar and restaurant a few miles north on Highway 101. The couple who ran it kept circus animals that they rented out to film and television companies; whenever the talk or music died down, it would be punctuated with roars from the lions, tigers, and elephants billeted below.

Olivia sat between us, chattering away with her usual abandon, while Anne and I took turns talking to her and ignoring each other. We continued to share a common existence and living space for a few more weeks, but it would be stretching a point to call us a couple any longer.

Anne made it clear she was leaving for Brazil whether I came or not. She never officially disinvited me, but as her departure date neared, I got the impression that changing my mind and joining her was no longer an option. On a sullen, chilly January day, I drove her to Willits, where she'd be catching the bus to San Francisco and points south.

We rode in near-silence, attempts at conversation dissolving into a gloomy, aching lack of anything left to talk about. Anne, her usually sunny disposition even then only partially obscured by clouds, made half-hearted references to how beautiful every-thing would be when she returned in the spring, but it was brutally obvious to both of us that she wouldn't be coming back.

I pulled up at the bus stop and stared out my window, refusing to acknowledge her attempts to say goodbye. "Um, okay, then," she finally said, "I guess I'll see you later." She opened the door and stepped out of my life.

five

five

While it was happening, and for a long time afterward, there was no doubt in my mind that 1985 was the worst year of my life. I wandered through it like a wounded animal, in so much darkness and pain that it would be well into the next decade, if not the next century, before I realized how nearly everything that happened that year played a part in altering my life forever, in ways I never could have begun to foresee.

It didn't start out as badly as it might have. Sad as I was about Anne leaving, I dealt with it at first by turning my grief into anger. How dare she desert me, I grumbled, just when the going got rough? How could she leave me to scrounge through another mountain winter while she lolled about on the beach in Rio?

It was a hard winter, too; not a ton of snow, but what there was turned to ice early on and stayed that way until spring. The roads were a treacherous nightmare, and the colder than usual nighttime temperatures made it a constant struggle to keep the house warm. The pipes froze and broke half a dozen times, leaving me without water and forcing me to spend hours crawling under the house with a flashlight, wrench, and hacksaw.

I brooded, seethed, totted up the injustices of the world. That kept me busy for the first few weeks. Then I decided to channel my energies into finishing the second issue of the *Iron Peak Lookout*.

I pounded away at the typewriter until I had filled six pages, two more than *Lookout* #1 had contained. With money in ever shorter supply, the extra printing costs were a problem, but I wasn't going to let that stop me. I was on a mission, and the world was going to hear about it. Whether it wanted to or not.

Having loved newspapers all my life, I was still reeling from the discovery that many people were not in love with mine. "When I decided to publish the *Lookout*," I understatedly editorialized in the new issue, "I expected it would cause some controversy."

But, I went on, I was appalled to find that what people objected to most was not what I was saying, but that it was being said at all. "The advantages of an informed community outweigh the dangers posed by a greater awareness of our existence," I argued, pointing out that those who wished to do us harm knew perfectly well what went on up here in the hills.

This sounded reasonable to me, but to the *Lookout*'s enemies, it was like waving the proverbial red rag at an already irate bull. The ink had barely cooled when I started hearing that I had better "watch my step."

I might have been more afraid if these warnings had been delivered directly instead of via the rumor mill, but I was spending most of my time alone, leaving my land only when necessary. This was not so much out of fear as from the feeling that, as a single man, I was no longer as welcome among my friends and neighbors as I'd been when I was part of a couple.

Long before Anne left, I'd heard stories about what happened to mountain men who lost their wives or girlfriends. "They sit up there getting crazier and crazier," someone once told me, "year after year, at first drinking a little too much and then drinking way too much, until they can't talk to anyone but themselves, and eventually they can't even manage that."

I'd met men matching this description, who the moment they spotted me would launch into an endless, convoluted version of the exact same story they'd told me the last ten times I'd seen them. Fearful of ending up the same way, I cut back dramatically on my own drinking and drug use. This would have been a good idea in any event, but the absence of liquid and chemical anesthesia left me that much more painfully aware of how dismal my life was becoming.

But was it really that bad? True, for the first time in years I had serious money troubles, even having to calculate whether I could afford the couple gallons of gas required for a trip to town and back. And though it ebbed and flowed, the dull, aching pain of being alone, of wondering when, or if, that solitude would ever end, never entirely left me.

Yet I'd felt that way before, been this poor before, been convinced my life had reached a dead end. Always in the past, something or someone had come along to renew my hope and courage. Why should it be any different this time?

It wasn't as if I had nothing to live for. Not only was I turning the *Iron Peak Lookout* into a "real" (at least in my own mind) newspaper, but my long-deferred dream of singing and playing in a punk rock band still had a chance of coming true.

Kain was making progress on the bass, even more so now that practice sessions weren't constantly interrupted by Anne and me fighting. All we were missing was a drummer. The marine-pearl Beatles-style Ludwig kit sat glistening in the corner of the practice room, waiting for someone to bring it to life. Somewhere, if not on this mountain then maybe the next, there had to be such a person.

I thought about everyone I knew. They didn't have to know anything about drumming. This was punk rock. Anyone capable of banging out a half-assed rhythm would do. I still couldn't think of who might fit that bill until I had one of those brainstorms that you laugh off at first because it seems so ridiculous, but if you think about it long enough, starts to make a certain inexorable sense.

It was a gloomy, bone-chilling day in early February. A vicious north wind spat bits of icy snow at my kitchen window as I nursed a cup of coffee and stared sullenly at the bleak, barren hills. That was when the idea popped into my head: Frank and Linda's 12-year-old son Tre supposedly had some musical talent.

Or so people said. He'd had lessons on several instruments—most recently the violin—and while never sticking with any of them, had a knack for quickly picking up the basics. He was also rambunctious, exuberant, and impossible to shut up; his CB handle was "Motormouth." (Mine was "Thrasher" and Anne's had been "Basher.") These were qualities I had come to believe were essential in a drummer.

Actual drumming ability or experience never seemed like that big a deal to me. Which was just as well, because Tre had never touched a drum in his life. Like many guitarists and singers, I had no idea how crucial the rhythm section is to a band's success. At the time, in fact, I'm not sure I even knew what a rhythm section was. Anyone capable of being as loud, crazy, and obnoxious as I wanted our band to be was welcome to join. Looked at in that light, Tre seemed like the perfect candidate. He had the added advantage of being the only one remotely interested in giving it a try.

Kain was not keen on the idea. In fact, he was dead set against it, even threatening to quit the band. It would be embarrassing, he argued. Nobody would take us seriously with a 12-year-old drummer. I'd had similar doubts, but quickly dismissed them.

"Nobody takes us seriously anyway," I reminded him. "Besides, we already have a 14-year-old; what difference is it going to make if we have a 12-year-old?"

"Big difference," Kain insisted. "A 12-year-old is still a little kid."

It had been a long time since I'd been Kain's age, too long for me to understand why he'd feel self-conscious about being seen hanging out with a kid two years his junior. So while he was away on a family trip, I decided to give Tre a tryout. If it worked, I reasoned, Kain would come around, and if it didn't, he never needed to know about it.

The night before Tre was scheduled to come over for his first practice, I was awakened around midnight by an engine's rumble and the crunch of tires on my frozen driveway. Headlights swept through the bedroom window and across the ceiling, and I wondered what sort of trouble might be on its way. People didn't make social calls that time of night.

A vehicle pulled up in front of the house, stopped, and cut off its lights and engine. I sat in the dark, not knowing whether to go for the flashlight or the shotgun. Then I heard Olivia's slightly querulous cry.

"Larry? Larry? Are you here, Larry?"

Sticking my head out the window, I saw her standing at my door, suitcase in hand. The car she'd arrived in looked like that of Jeff, my increasingly no-account brother-in-common-law. Before I could open the door to let Olivia in, he turned and drove away.

Huffing, puffing, and cursing in that grande dame-cum-working girl accent of hers, Olivia let me know what she thought of Jeff. "A bastard, that one," she declaimed, "a right proper bastard."

She was never one for skimping on the epithets, but tonight Olivia swore with a fervor that couldn't quite hide how upset she was. I made her a cup of tea while, in between barrages of invective, she told me what had happened.

Jeff's "business" deals often kept him away for days or weeks at a time, leaving my sister and her kids—there were three now, with a fourth about to be born—to fend for themselves, sometimes with no food or money, and with no idea when—or if—he'd be back.

When he did re-appear, usually toting a suitcase full of cash, life would turn from famine to feast. If anyone complained about his absence, he'd let a look of deep hurt play across his face—which uncannily resembled that of a basset hound—and say something to the effect of, "But look at all the presents I brought you!"

Olivia, who'd been staying with my sister, was not impressed with this routine, and didn't hesitate to let Jeff know about it. Accustomed to ruling his roost with absolute authority, Jeff was even less impressed with Olivia's freely and frequently offered views on his shortcomings.

So most likely he'd been looking for a pretext to get rid of her anyway when she innocently—or so she claimed—used one of his vegetarian-only pans for a meat-laden fry-up. The ensuing discussion escalated into a shouting match, ending with her insisting on being taken to my house in the middle of the night, unwilling to spend another minute under the roof of "that bloody awful man."

We decided—well, she decided, not that I wasn't happy to have her—that she'd be staying with me from now on. Which was how she happened to be there, cowering in the upstairs bedroom, when I introduced Tre to the drums and gave him his first lesson.

I should add that I myself didn't know the first thing about playing drums. But I'd developed a theory, or at least a hunch, that in order to avoid the kind of conflicts I'd had with Anne, it would be best to keep things simple. Very simple.

I removed the cymbals and all the drums except for the kick and the snare, and told Tre to try playing the most fundamental of beats to my fuzzy, punked up version of Danny and the Juniors' 50s classic "At The Hop." After an hour or so of that, we moved on to the virtually identical "Rock And Roll Is Here To Stay."

We were a little ramshackle and shambolic, but I thought it sounded good. Good enough, anyway. Not so Olivia, who didn't hesitate to let me know that it had been "the most godawful racket" she'd ever heard in her life.

I could see how it might sound that way to her, but then she wasn't trying to start a punk rock band. What mattered was that Tre had been a) eager to learn and b) clearly capable of keeping a beat. Hell, on his first day, he was already better at it than me.

I invited him to join the band, and decided that his punk name, playing on the resemblance of "Tre" to "*très*"—French for "very"—would be Tre Cool. We started practicing several times a week; luckily for Olivia, the weather had warmed up enough that she could go for long walks to seek refuge from our—another favorite description of hers—"infernal noise."

Despite her age—she was 67 at the time—Olivia loved rock and roll, which in her mind meant the 50s-style rock and roll Tre and I focused on at first. But she couldn't understand or tolerate what we were doing to it. Years later, when Tre had gone on to fame and fortune as one of the world's best drummers, I was sitting with Olivia in her London flat watching him perform on TV with his new band, Green Day.

"Remember when he used to come over to the house to practice?" I asked her. Harrumphing, she made a sour face to remind me what she had thought of it. A couple days later Tre stopped by for a visit, and greeted Olivia with, "Hey, guess what? I finally got a job playing drums! They even pay me!"

"All well and good," she said, "and I'm very pleased for you. But I still maintain that what you and Larry were playing back on the mountain was the most godawful racket I ever heard in my life."

But at last we had a band, or would as soon as Kain got home from his trip. In the meantime, I pounded out issue #3 of the *Iron Peak Lookout*, the biggest yet, and, as it turned out, the last to be published under that name.

On a bright, mild day that hinted at an early spring, half a dozen unhappy-looking mountain men came striding up my driveway.

"We need to talk to you about that newspaper of yours," said the tallest of them, a normally genial guy who everyone knew as Teepee Doug, thanks to his having lived for the last several years in a hand-built teepee near the bottom of the Loop.

"There's nothing to talk about. It's gotta stop! Right now!" squeaked the troll-like, bearded little hippie they called Tree Danny. He'd gotten that name from being widely suspected— though it was never proved—of cutting down an old-growth fir at the bottom end of my property for no apparent reason other than pure malice. He harbored a special hatred toward me because I'd been heard making fun of the Grateful Dead.

Danny would get red in the face and shake uncontrollably when he was angry. I'd heard the expression "hopping mad" before, but never fully understood it until—in response to my saying something about the First Amendment and freedom of the press—he literally started jumping up and down and sputtering with rage.

"It's a long way to town," he hissed through clenched teeth. "A guy's house could catch fire real easy."

This was true. Living alone left me especially vulnerable.

Sooner or later I'd have to leave my house, and even the quickest trip to Laytonville for groceries and supplies took a couple of hours. A lot could happen in that time, and Danny looked more than crazy enough to see that it did.

Teepee Doug tried to cool things down, but said he couldn't be responsible for what somebody else might do if I didn't at least try to compromise. Feeling as if I didn't have much choice, I agreed to stop writing about pot growing in our immediate area and to remove the "Iron Peak" name and logo from my masthead.

Issue #4, in April of 1985, was renamed the *Mendocino Mountain Lookout*, and June's issue, #6, became just plain *Lookout*. The June issue also began looking less like a newspaper and more like a magazine or zine. Some people mischaracterized it as a fanzine, but I found that annoying since I wasn't really a fan of much.

I filled the front cover of #6 with a crude collage of newspaper headlines, the first time I'd tried incorporating "art" into the *Lookout*. I began writing about subjects far afield from Spy Rock and the Emerald Triangle—the latter being the newly popular name for our region, originally coined by a CAMP spokesperson to evoke comparisons with Southeast Asia's opium-producing Golden Triangle.

Thus emerged the curious—some even called it schizophrenic—mixture of urban punk rock and politics with rural news, gossip, and environmentalism that would enchant some readers and vex others for as long as the *Lookout* existed. If the *Ledger* hadn't refused to print my letters, I might never have started the *Lookout*; if not for my vigilante neighbors, I might never have expanded my scope beyond agricultural reports, mudslides, and bear invasions. Seen in that light, I suppose they both did me a favor.

It was a grim, leaden-skied day in March when I showed up to collect the mail from my post office box in town and found it overflowing with letters—and checks—from people all over the country who wanted to subscribe to the *Lookout*. Unbeknownst to me, Alexander Cockburn had quoted one of my articles in his column in *The Nation*.

Until then, I'd never thought of the *Lookout* as something people would be willing to pay for. I quickly had to re-assess that view and come up with a pricing structure for subscribers. Around the same time, I received a letter of praise from one of my longtime heroes, the *San Francisco Chronicle*'s Herb Caen. While still barely tolerated on my own mountain, I was gaining admirers in faraway—and highly regarded—places.

The new money coming in enabled me to expand my print run and to distribute additional copies of the *Lookout* up and down the coast and in the Bay Area. By summer I could brag that I had outstripped the *Laytonville Ledger* in both size and circulation.

But while the *Lookout* was enjoying more success than I'd ever dreamed of, our band was still struggling to get off the ground. After some initial griping, Kain had accepted Tre as our drummer, and eventually even admitted—if a bit grudgingly— that the kid wasn't half bad. But though we'd managed to put a few songs together, we still didn't even have a name for the band. Kain and Tre dismissed every one of my suggestions as dumb or embarrassing, but never offered any alternatives.

In light of the magazine's recently gained notoriety, I thought it might be smart to stick with the same theme and call ourselves the Lookouts. Tre and Kain hated that one, too, but after a few days of bickering, I set a deadline for them to come up with a better suggestion. They didn't, and Lookouts it would be.

We took photos of ourselves on the back deck, on the assumption that the world would soon be clamoring to see what we looked like. Our first "show" took place that summer, during the annual Fourth of July party. We were nowhere near ready for a public unveiling, but most of the friends, neighbors, and relatives who watched us were too polite to say so.

Now it was time to make a demo tape. Most new bands start out by recording their best three or four songs, maybe a couple more if they're really ambitious. We did 22, some of which we'd learned the day before going into the studio, a converted garage outside of Willits. It was run by a guy named Hal Wagenet, who'd played guitar for the 60s band It's a Beautiful Day and had the gold record on his wall to prove it.

Wagenet was pleasant enough, while not bothering to hide the fact that he didn't think much of our band. But he let us down in a big way by neglecting to tell us we were badly out of tune for the whole second half of the session. "I assumed that's how you wanted it," he said as we listened to the playback. At that point, we had neither the time nor money to go back and fix it.

Granted, it was our responsibility as "musicians" to tune our instruments and be aware of how we sounded. Strictly speaking, Wagenet had no obligation to help us out in that department. But it came across as a rather mean-spirited bit of hippie passive-aggressiveness, the sort of thing you often ran into around Mendocino County. Wagenet later went on to serve a couple terms as County Supervisor, giving him the opportunity to similarly exasperate quite a few more people.

Having learned that expensive lesson, we limped back to our mountain lair with a sadly flawed tape that nonetheless managed to capture something of what we were about. I sent a copy to *Maximum Rocknroll*, the de facto clearinghouse and pre-eminent voice of the international punk rock scene. Editor/publisher Tim Yohannan shocked us by giving it a rave review.

I would later learn that Tim practiced a form of affirmative action, giving especially favorable treatment to bands from remote or unusual places. As the first band to send in a demo from the backwoods of Northern California, we had almost certainly benefited from this policy.

At the time, though, the review was enough to convince us we were headed for punk rock superstardom. I immediately set up our first official show in the parking lot of Czech Lodge, a general store and mountain hangout located on Highway 101, a mile north of the Spy Rock turnoff.

We played to a mixture of hippies who would show up for anything that promised a chance to "boogie" and some vaguely New Wave-ish fans of The Front, a Laytonville band I'd invited to headline in hopes of attracting an audience beyond the same friends, neighbors, and relatives who'd watched our Fourth of July show.

I was so nervous that I was barely able to look at the crowd, let alone get an accurate picture of what they might be thinking. Then one audience member—a boozy, bearded musician who went by the name of Piano Jimmy—made his feelings clear by stalking up to the stage and pulling the plug on us halfway through our medley of the Velvet Underground's "Heroin" and the Rolling Stones' "You Can't Always Get What You Want."

"That's not music, it's just a bunch of noise," he shouted, echoing an opinion I'd been hearing from my father ever since I discovered rock and roll in the 1950s. Cooler heads prevailed over Jimmy to let us finish our set, but afterward I found that he was far from being the only non-fan. I don't know what I'd been thinking, but songs like "Fuck Religion" and "Fourth Reich

(Nazi Amerika)" hadn't won us many new friends, especially among parents of the young children in attendance.

Tre himself was still only 12 and looked, if anything, younger, making for a jarring juxtaposition when he added his angelic soprano vocals to our cacophonous barrage of anger and vitriol. Fortunately Frank and Linda, while not necessarily fans of our sound, remained bemusedly tolerant of their son's new hobby. Other parents, though, expressed outrage that I was "forcing," or at least encouraging, "that little boy" to say such vile things.

The crowd wasn't keen on my anti-hippie anthems either, especially "My Mom Smokes Pot" ("She smokes it a lot, she's really quite mellow, but her brains are like jello"). In real life, none of our band's mothers were big pot smokers, but plenty of other moms were, and they didn't appreciate their "sacrament" being ridiculed.

I, however, was always looking for ways to inflame the masses, and realized I had hit upon a winner. From then on, whether in *Lookout* magazine or writing songs for the band, I never neglected an opportunity to take a shot at the smugness and self-indulgence of hippie culture, even if by some standards I still resembled a hippie myself.

In fact, economic necessity had finally forced me into becoming—or at least trying to become—something I'd sworn I'd never be: a marijuana farmer. With any money that came in going to finance the magazine and band, I looked on track to be dead broke by winter if I didn't find a new source of income.

I knew next to nothing about growing, and wished I'd paid more attention to how Anne had gone about it, but how hard could it be? You threw some seeds in the ground, watered them, and waited for the money to roll in, right?

It turned out to be a little more complicated than that. It also became painfully obvious that illegal agriculture was not one of my talents. From the start, almost everything that could go wrong did. Other farmers were nurturing plants six feet tall while I was still trying to coax the wrong kind of seedlings from an unproductive blend of soil.

Rats gnawed holes in my water lines, the pump failed, a series of blazing hot days threatened to turn the land into my own private dust bowl, and, upping the level of my tribulations to near-Biblical scale, a plague of locusts (well, grasshoppers, which apparently are more or less the same thing) descended and began devouring everything in sight.

Through it all, and with numbing despair as my near-constant companion, I managed to keep my plants alive; the one saving grace was that they were too tiny to spot from the air when the CAMP planes and helicopters arrived. Most of Spy Rock was counting the days until harvest time while I hoped against hope that some of my crop might reach maturity before the first freeze.

October stayed blessedly warm and dry, which helped, but toward the end of the month the temperature plummeted and an early blizzard blew in. Dragging myself out of bed before dawn, I crawled into the woods with a flashlight to cut down my plants before the snow destroyed them. I salvaged three or four ounces of substandard product; I'd been hoping for three or four pounds. When sold, it netted me slightly less than it had cost to grow.

My fussing over magazines and bands and money and abortive pot harvests never completely obscured the deepening pall that solitude and Anne's absence had cast over the year. I'd seen her once, in mid-spring, when she'd shown up to collect her belongings. Before I thought to ask, she said, "You realize I'm not coming back, don't you?"

She stayed two days, which was how long it took to load

everything into her pickup. I watched her drive away, the truck so weighed down that it struggled to navigate the road's more prominent ruts and potholes. When the last echo of her engine's whine vanished behind the mountain and the dust cloud she'd left in her wake dwindled down to imperceptibility, I went inside and sat down on the drum stool in the chilly, lifeless band room.

"Well, Larry," I said out loud, startling myself with the sound of my own voice, "you've finally got what you wanted. You're completely and utterly alone." Then I broke into great racking sobs that filled most of what remained of the afternoon.

The house felt shockingly empty. I took to pacing from room to room, up the stairs and down again, then plopping myself in front of the piano and squinting by candlelight—the solar panels still worked, but the batteries were failing, and I needed to save electricity for band practice—at the sheet music I was using to teach myself every sad and lovelorn torch song ever written.

Things were going wrong physically, too. I was developing strange rashes, something that looked like it might be shingles, and horrible cold sores that festered into gaping cancerous-looking wounds. I was 37, almost 38, an age that seemed so advanced to 14-year-old Kain that he observed, "You'll probably never find another girlfriend."

I became obsessed with the idea that I'd been infected with AIDS or some similarly deadly disease, and that I'd probably never make it to 40. If it weren't for the band, the magazine, and my recurring fantasies that something great still lay ahead, I would have been fine with that.

My youngest brother drove up from the Bay Area and surprised me on my birthday, the first visitor I'd had from the outside world in longer than I cared to remember. We sat in silence, picking at a pound cake he'd picked up at the gas station in Laytonville. A single candle lit the room, not just to save electricity, but because I didn't want him to notice an especially bad cold sore that had just flared up.

Shadows played across the walls; a stinging early winter wind rattled loose windowpanes and caused the house to creak and sigh. The last autumn leaves, along with various twigs and pinecones, attacked the roof with enough force to sound like fitful bursts of rain. My brother could see I was hurting and desperate, but I'm not sure he grasped the full extent of what I was feeling. I'd always been his big, know-it-all brother, the guy with an answer for everything.

Most of that had been a bluff, of course. The difference was that in the past, even when I'd been privately terrified or befuddled, I'd been able to put on a brave enough front to fool at least some people into thinking I knew what I was doing. Now I was no longer able to fool anyone, least of all myself. I was out of answers, out of hope, out of time.

six

six

Winter came in hard that year, and stayed hard. By mid-December it was obvious I had nowhere near enough firewood to last until spring. I struggled to replenish my supply, but with so few daylight hours—not to mention ice and snow clinging tenaciously to everything, making much of the land impassable—it felt like a losing battle.

I should have cut and seasoned more wood the previous spring and summer, but I'd wasted too much time moping around, and feeling sorry for myself. I had accomplished one major feat, though: laying 2,000 feet of pipe over the hills to connect my water tank with a previously unused well at the far end of my property.

The well had been there all along but for the first few years it had been easier to get water from the creek than to go to the effort and expense of developing it. As more people moved in upstream, though, I could no longer rely on creek water being safe to drink. Human sewage, as well as the bear droppings that seemed to be showing up more often these days, made it increasingly likely to carry the intestinal parasite known as giardia.

Besides, I'd had enough of trying to keep the pump going through the dry season and to prevent it from being destroyed by mud, water, and rocks over the winter. So my mini-version of the California Water Project—the series of canals and pumps that had diverted Northern California's water southward and made Los Angeles possible—was one thing I did that year that tangibly improved my quality of life.

Part of the job involved rolling a 1,200-gallon water tank—by myself, I note—to the top of the highest hill on the property. From there, the law of gravity provided me with water pressure rivaling or surpassing what you'd find in town. I had to replace all my plumbing fittings with stronger ones, but once that was done, my garden hose could direct a stream of water all the way onto the roof in case of fire. Or if, you know, I felt like washing my shingles.

Still, after the year I'd had, the prospect of another long mountain winter was deeply disheartening. So when a friend offered me the use of her room in San Francisco while she went traveling, I jumped at the chance. I felt like a deserter, but after four unbroken years on the mountain, I was ready for at least a temporary change.

The apartment was in a desolate, little traveled corner of the city, above a bar called the Bottom of the Hill. A few years later, this bar would become a popular music venue, but at the beginning of 1986 it was a middle-aged alcoholics' hangout, dismissed by my roommates and myself as the "Bottom of the Barrel."

It had been years since I'd last lived in San Francisco. I wasn't sure which had changed more, the city or me, but I felt as though I'd dropped in from another time and space, maybe even another dimension. Most people I'd known there were gone; quite a few, thanks to the AIDS virus then running rampant, were dead.

The apartment was the kind of bare-bones setup where you'd expect to find the struggling artists and musicians who'd all but disappeared from the city's more opulent quarters. Unheated, apart from the warmth that could be coaxed from the kitchen stove and oven, it still offered what felt like the unspeakable luxury of being able to stay up late reading or writing under electric lights that didn't rely on fading batteries, or being able to walk to the kitchen to make a phone call instead of driving 10 miles down to the highway.

Much of the street life I'd once loved about San Francisco seemed to have vanished. What was left was far across town. I could see lights beckoning in the distance, shockingly bright compared with the stars, moonlight, and dimly adumbrated mountaintops that filled the Spy Rock skies. But like a desert mirage, what promise they held seemed to evaporate before I could reach them.

Many people speak of San Francisco in the 80s as a halcyon era; to me it felt like a ghost town, a graveyard for a dream. I remembered why I'd left the city to start my own version of civilization in the wilderness, but after the year I'd just endured in the country, I felt hamstrung between two equally untenable worlds.

Anyway, I hadn't really escaped from Spy Rock. At least once a week I had to travel north to feed Ruf-Ruf, Kong, and the four (or was it six now?) cats. City people found it shocking—and seldom hesitated to tell me so—that I would leave the animals on their own, with nothing to sustain them but a 50 pound bag of dog food (it was cheaper than cat food and looked to be made of pretty much the same stuff).

"Won't they eat all the food and then go hungry till you come back?" "Don't they get lonely?" "Where will they sleep if you're not there to let them in the house?"

I could never seem to make them understand that these animals were not pets. On the contrary, I considered them working partners in Livermore Acres. My job was to feed them, theirs to stand guard (dogs) and to keep the snake and rat population under control (cats).

They lived outdoors year round, whether 1 was home or not, and ate only when they were hungry, so it was no problem leaving a week's worth of food for them at a time. As for whether they were "lonely," 1 can't claim to be an animal mind reader or psychologist. They looked pleased to see me when 1 was around, but seemed equally content with their own company.

On especially cold nights, 1 might invite them in to sit a spell by the fire, but they'd always be herded back outdoors before 1 went to bed. 1 didn't want to pamper them, nor did 1 want to grow too attached. I'd been warned when 1 picked up our first two kittens that mountain cats seldom enjoyed a long life or comfortable old age. There were too many things out there bigger, stronger, and hungrier than they were.

So far all my cats and dogs had managed to avoid the various mountain lions, bobcats, hawks, owls, coyotes, and bears that might have made a quick meal of them. They met their match, however, when a little old skunk took up residence in the crawl space under the house, which was where 1 left the animals' food, and where they slept on cold nights.

You can see why the skunk would find that setup attractive, but unfortunately, she wasn't willing to share. Any time the dogs or cats stuck their noses in, let alone came near their feed tray, she'd let loose with a blast of stink.

It took me a while to figure out what was going on. When 1 slept at Spy Rock I'd often be awakened by the essence of skunk wafting up through the floorboards. But as long as 1 was spending only one or two nights a week there, 1 shrugged it off as a minor inconvenience. It was only when 1 noticed how emaciated the dogs and cats were looking that 1 realized the skunk had completely commandeered their food supply.

Things got worse as winter wore on. The skunk grew big and fat, and 1 knew it would only be a matter of time before she invited friends, or possibly a skunk husband and some babies, to join the party. Between the dogs barking and the smell regularly filling the house, I could no longer get a decent night's sleep in my own bed. Something had to be done.

Trying to chase the skunk out by throwing things or shouting at it had produced no results, so my thoughts turned toward a more violent solution. I had a rifle and a shotgun, but given the ability of a run-over skunk to stink up a mile or so of highway, I suspected it wouldn't be a smart idea to blow one to smithereens underneath my house. Unfortunately, she seldom if ever felt the need to venture out from her comfortable hidey-hole, so I didn't see a lot of choices.

I'd blithely carried a pistol around during my teenage hoodlum days—managing only through the grace of God or sheer blind luck not to shoot myself or someone else—but I'd never bothered learning the proper use or care of firearms. I kept guns now only because the nearest sheriff's station was an hour away, not counting the 20 or 30 minutes it would take to reach a phone to call for help. When it came to dealing with predators, human or otherwise, we were on our own up here.

Shortly after moving into the house, I discovered—by nearly stepping into it—a colony of young rattlesnakes living under my front porch. Baby rattlers are particularly dangerous, because they haven't yet learned to limit the amount of venom they release when they bite. I decided a 200-yard perimeter around the house was going to be a snake-free zone.

I used my shovel to behead the little critters, and left their carcasses for the cats—still just kittens at the time—hoping it might help them acquire a taste for snake meat. It must have worked; once the cats were fully-grown, they hunted down, killed and ate any snake that ventured into the vicinity. In the meantime, though, I had an unhappy encounter with a much bigger snake—maybe five or six feet long—that I found straddling my driveway.

Afraid to get close enough to give it the shovel treatment, I got out the .22 and fired off half a dozen shots. Most of them missed; the one or two that hit home barely seemed to trouble him.

So I tried the shotgun. From that distance, even I couldn't miss. The snake flopped around a bit, and I let go a second blast that shredded it to pieces. Only then did I discover that it hadn't been a rattlesnake at all. Instead, I'd killed a harmless gopher snake.

Still new to the mountains, and still in thrall to a hippie-cum-Disney view of nature, I was beside myself with remorse at having needlessly exterminated a beautiful woodland creature. I put the guns back in the cupboard, where they'd remained until the skunk affair drove me to the brink of distraction.

Lying in the snow at 2 am in mid-January, flashlight in one hand and rifle in the other, I no longer harbored such compunctions. I was ready to become a cold-blooded killer. The skunk came meandering out from behind a foundation post, eyes glowing a vivid orange in the flashlight's beam as she stared nonchalantly back at me.

Gritting my teeth, I pulled the trigger. My marksmanship hadn't improved since my snake-shooting days; the skunk stood looking at me as if to say, "And your point is...?" Two more shots with the .22 accomplished nothing; seemingly bored with this business, she began to wander away.

All right then, I said, reaching for the shotgun.

The sound of the blast, trapped as it was within the confines of the crawl space, was as ear-splitting as it was terrifying, but the skunk was no longer going anywhere, except possibly to skunk heaven. The smell was overpowering, and would remain so for a few days. But that was a minor detail compared with the adrenaline rush I experienced.

The sensation was partly one of relief at having put an end to an exasperating problem, but there was more to it than that. I felt an almost savage exhilaration at having killed—obliterated, really—my first mammal. I remembered feeling this way once before, when, shortly after I'd begun studying martial arts, I used my newly acquired skill to backhand a barroom drinking buddy who'd been giving me grief.

The visceral sensation of power and triumph at the sight of the blood I'd drawn gave way to a sickening plummet into remorse and shame. I wasn't the sort of person who took pleasure in hurting or killing things. Or was I? Oscillating between the two extremes of emotion, then as now, kept me wide awake for the rest of the night.

Ruf-Ruf and Kong, their long winter nightmare finally over, showed no such ambivalence. Without waiting for the smell to die down, they devoured every edible part of the skunk and spent the next few weeks playing with its hide, sending it back and forth across the snow with their noses like a hockey puck or soccer ball.

Every so often they'd interrupt their game to attack, with great menacing growls, the few tufts of fur that remained, as if to assure themselves it was still dead. Well into spring I was still finding bits of black and white hair scattered about the yard.

I came to terms with my role as judge, jury, and executioner of anything that disturbed the equilibrium of our little world. When, later that year, another skunk came wobbling erratically down the driveway in broad daylight—a likely sign it was suffering from rabies—I dispatched it without a moment's hesitation or sentiment.

It was a turning point of sorts. My life still sucked, at least as I self-pityingly saw it, but I was beginning to feel less like a victim, less overpowered by circumstances beyond my control.

My skunk adventures felt starkly at odds with the re-urbanization process I'd been undergoing in San Francisco. People there hardly knew what to make of my stories of mountain life. I got the impression they often didn't believe what I told them, that they thought of me as a colorful but essentially harmless lunatic.

Later that month, I ventured across the Bay to Emeryville for a show at the New Method warehouse, named for a long defunct laundry that had once occupied the space. I brought along copies of *Lookout* and was surprised to find people who were not only familiar with my magazine, but who'd been wondering who I was and were hoping to meet me.

Among them was a friendly if somewhat inquisitorial teenager by the name of Aaron Cometbus. I knew him by reputation; he'd been publishing the fanzine that had given him his surname de plume since he was 13. I'd found my first *Cometbus* on an empty seat while riding the 43 Masonic bus in San Francisco. Aaron told me he often left copies in random places in hopes somebody interesting might pick them up. I'd been doing the same thing with *Lookout*.

Aaron introduced me to Tim Yohannan, the fast-talking, wisecracking host of Maximum Rocknroll radio and editor/publisher of *Maximum Rocknroll* magazine. I'd been listening to his radio show, broadcast every Tuesday night on Berkeley's KPFA, on and off since the late 70s. I'd almost forgotten about the show during my first couple years on Spy Rock, until I discovered that if I parked at a certain spot on the ridge near the top of Iron Peak, I could pick it up loud and clear, even from 200 miles away.

I'd formed a mental image of Yohannan, based on his cackling laugh and the loud sardonic asides he delivered in between spinning that week's selection of newly minted punk rock records. I was expecting, unlikely as it might seem in mid-80s San Francisco, the sort of leather-jacketed greaser you'd find hanging out on a street corner in 1950s Brooklyn or Jersey. It turned out I'd been right about the motorcycle jacket and New Jersey, but apart from that Tim was nothing like the greasers I'd grown up with.

Obsessed with guitar-driven punk rock and garage music, but also a stone cold Marxist, he was extraordinarily knowledgeable on some subjects while remaining blithely, even deliberately, oblivious to others. In one epic argument he and I had about the value of education, Tim angrily declaimed, "I never learned a damn thing in college," to which I retorted, "Well, that much is obvious."

Although Tim and I would frequently butt heads in the coming years, he was very supportive of my early efforts. As a result of his reviews in *Maximum Rocknroll*, the Lookouts and *Lookout* magazine had gained more fans across the United States and in several foreign countries than we'd ever managed to attract back home in Mendocino County.

Apart from a handful of teenagers who liked our band and a few adults who appreciated the nonstop sarcasm and irascible name-calling that filled the *Lookout,* I remained distinctly unpopular with most of the local population. Not having a personal acquaintance with many of the people and institutions I wrote about, it never occurred to me that my insults and invective might do more than just ruffle feathers.

I hadn't yet learned to value the quaint custom—at least it seemed quaint to me—of being polite and courteous to those we disagree with. More to the point, I failed to understand how vital it is to maintain some degree of civility and tolerance in a small rural community, where the person you denounced or cursed out yesterday is likely to be standing in line with you at the general store or post office today.

When the pastor of the Community Christian Church called AIDS a divine punishment for sexual perversion—an opinion often heard at the time—I saw nothing wrong with calling him a moron and referring to his congregation as the "Community Cretin Church." When Bill Bailey, whose logging supplies business had made him Laytonville's richest man, spoke out against the environmental movement, I declared the journalistic equivalent of thermonuclear war.

A generous contributor to many community causes, Bailey was mostly well thought of. He was not universally loved, even among his employees, a couple of whom assisted me in my crusade by feeding me inside info about his shadier exploits. But the consensus among townspeople was that, warts and all, Bailey was "one of us," while I, the semi-anonymous and wildly intemperate voice from the remote reaches of Spy Rock, was most decidedly not.

At the same time, the once-gaping divide between "rednecks" and "hippies" was fading away as the two cultures interacted, intermarried, and did business together. Once content to sell land, soil, and plastic pipe to the hippies, old-timers jumped into the marijuana growing game themselves, while hippies sported cowboy boots, drove old pickup trucks, and let their accents morph into a half-country, half-western drawl.

"We're from North California and South Alabam," Hank Williams, Jr. sang in "A Country Boy Can Survive," the strident paean to down home ways that had been a big part of the soundtrack to my first year on the mountain. My dad, never a fan of Southern music or dialects, made the same comparison.

"You're living like a bunch of hillbillies up here," he would gripe. I allowed that there was a lot of "y'all" and "I reckon" emanating from the mouths of city-bred folk like myself, but I didn't see anything wrong with that. Like others before me, I figured it was just the mountain version of "When in Rome..."

There were newcomers who took things further, sauntering around with six-shooters—or the modern equivalent—strapped to their belts. One wild-eyed hippie, typically seen with his tangled mane trailing in the breeze as he tore around the back roads on a high-powered dirt bike, exacted frontier justice after coming out on the wrong end of an unhappy love triangle by shooting his rival's horse.

Another mountain stalwart, whose family occupied a Dogpatchian cluster of shacks and hovels on an otherwise barren hillside, was arrested for having sex with his daughters and fathering a child with one of them. It had been going on for years before anyone thought to notify the authorities. He was also alleged to have shot his teenaged son ("only in the arm," his defenders pointed out) to teach him a lesson when the boy started showing a similarly unhealthy interest in his sisters.

This was one of the few occasions when someone breached the "see no evil" attitude that permeated Spy Rock. As a rule, no matter how heinous a crime you witnessed, calling the sheriff about it was worse. This was partly due to a general distrust of and distaste for authority of any kind. People who move 20 miles out into the wilderness don't tend to be law and order fanatics.

But most of all, it was marijuana that covered a multitude of sins. Nuisances, annoyances, even environmental outrages were tolerated, ignored, or hushed up because nobody wanted to give the police an excuse to come sniffing around. When one grower's chemical fertilizer spilled into the creek and turned it a shocking bright orange, I expected people downstream, especially those whose drinking water was threatened, to be up in arms.

Barely a word was said about it. "It'll clear up in a few days," was the predominant view. Even those who admitted it was out of line to use dangerous chemicals near a vital water source would have considered it far worse to put the errant grower at risk of being busted by reporting the spill to the county.

In an attempt to evade the prying eyes of the CAMP raiders, many farmers had taken their crops indoors, into barns, sheds, or underground bunkers, where they used artificial lights powered by heavy-duty diesel generators. When I returned from my San Francisco hiatus, I was shocked to find the once almost perfect stillness of the mountain shattered by an engine's roar and whine.

I assumed someone—as near as I could tell, the sound was coming from a neighbor's place down the hill—was doing construction work and would soon shut things down for the night, but the engine was still running when I fell into an uneasy sleep, and when I awoke the following morning. Even with my doors and windows closed, I could hear it loud and clear.

It went on like that, 24 hours a day, for the next year and a half, with only the briefest of interruptions when they'd turn it off for maintenance or refueling. Neighbors on two other sides of me also began running generators fulltime. Making it especially maddening, they'd locate them somewhere down a hillside where their own homes would be shielded from the racket while I got the full brunt of it.

The relentless noise was the most noticeable—and irritating—part of the problem, but there were other issues. Generator-powered grows often operated on the scale of full-fledged industrial facilities, which in an urban area would be subject to inspection and regulation. But up here there was no one to ensure that diesel fuel wasn't leaking into the ground water or that fire safety precautions were being observed.

It was early summer when the first generator exploded. Thankfully the woods and grass hadn't dried out yet, or the whole mountainside might have gone up in smoke. As it was, flames went leaping at least a hundred feet into the air, attracting the attention of Department of Forestry firefighters, who, on discovering the origin of the blaze, called in the sheriff to arrest those responsible.

Police involvement in such situations, however, was a rarity. Although generator fires became common, people usually managed to extinguish them without outside assistance. Neighbors worried that one of the explosions could erupt into a full-fledged forest fire, and some, like me, complained that the constant roar of diesel engines made it feel more like we were living in the parking lot of a truck stop than in the middle of the wilderness.

But nothing was going to be done about it. Nobody would file a noise or hazardous materials complaint, for fear it would escalate into a marijuana bust that could send someone to prison for years.

Indoor growing exacted another kind of toll on the community, dividing growers into separate classes, one of which was energy and chemical-intensive—factory farming in the most literal sense of the term—while the other employed traditional, often organic, agricultural methods. It was widely agreed that outdoor-grown marijuana possessed a superior flavor and character, but the indoor stuff could be just as powerfully psychedelic, and fetched a similar price.

The indoor growers had a couple of big advantages. Their costs were higher, but they could produce crops year round, while nature restricted outdoor growers to a single growing season. And outdoor crops were far more likely to attract the attention of CAMP spotter planes.

One neighbor, among the first to switch to indoor growing, used his profits to buy a bulldozer and dump truck; fueled by a steady diet of cocaine and amphetamines, he spent his days and often his nights excavating bunkers to further expand his operation. By the time he dropped dead from overwork and drug abuse, he had carved out an underground labyrinth that dwarfed his above-ground home, and was said to be grossing a million dollars a year.

During the last year of his life he seldom if ever left his land. He couldn't afford to. Outdoor growers had a wide range of places where they could hide their plants; if one of those spots was discovered, it was easy enough to dig new holes somewhere else. Indoor grows, on the other hand, were limited to one or two easily located buildings.

Once people knew where his crop was—and word spread fast on the mountain—the indoor grower became a hostage to his fortune. He or one of his cronies had to keep watch constantly. Letting their guard down for a moment could cost tens, even hundreds of thousands of dollars.

My hostility toward the indoor growing scene was an example of how I sometimes found myself sharply at odds with my neighbors. Underlying this conflict was my somewhat self-centered assumption that any reasonable person, if they thought about it, would see things the same way I did.

Saving the trees, protecting the ground water, building sustainable communities that weren't reliant on fossil fuels: these seemed like self-evidently good causes. I had a hard time accepting that for some people, making large sums of money was an even better one.

It was a long while before I understood that just because my neighbors and I led similar lifestyles, we weren't necessarily on the same page politically or environmentally. I was disappointed to find that at heart some hippies were not all that different from the corporations that were busily stripping Mendocino County of its last salable redwoods. Instead of accepting that, just as in the city, people came in all sizes, shapes, and stripes of opinion, I railed against them as if they were criminals.

This simplistic sort of thinking got me into trouble time and again. By reducing complex situations and people to slogans and formulas, I undermined my ability to get along and form alliances. The punks saw it differently: as far as they were concerned, the more outrageous and obnoxious I got, the better. But no matter how much time I spent hanging out with the punks down in the city, I eventually had to come home to the mountain, where I was not exactly Mr. Popularity.

I was acquiring a handful of supportive local readers, though. One of them, hearing through the grapevine about my financial troubles and my ludicrous lack of success at growing marijuana, offered to give me a hand with the coming year's crop. Her biggest contribution, in addition to a great deal of wise advice, was to supply me with a couple dozen greenhouse-grown plants—at five feet tall, already larger than mine had been at harvest time the previous season—to put into the ground in the second week of May.

All I had to do was transport them from one end of the county to the other, which meant piloting an ungainly moving van through the 50-mile gauntlet of Highway 101, a stretch perennially staked out by dope-hunting sheriff's deputies and CHP officers. The reek of cannabis emanating from the rear of my van was so powerful that getting stopped for a routine traffic violation or safety check would have instantly spelled curtains. While waiting at a traffic light in downtown Willits, I saw pedestrians sniffing the air and smirking in my direction.

It was one of the most hair-raising journeys of my life, rivaled only by a 100-mile carom through the mountains of Western Pennsylvania in a whiteout blizzard back in 1968, with both driver and myself high on a mega-dose of LSD. But I made it home to Spy Rock, and the plants, specially bred by my benefactor to flourish in this terrain and climate, did exceptionally well.

Having some significant income for the first time since 1982 left me free to devote more time to the band and magazine. The Lookouts played our first shows in the Bay Area that year, and were far better received than we'd ever been in Mendocino County. *Lookout* magazine continued to grow, too; my circulation doubled, then doubled again.

This newfound semi-prosperity allowed me to rent a room in San Francisco again the following winter. For the next year and a half I'd find myself pushed and pulled between two homes, rural and urban. Unable or unwilling to choose between them, I lived in constant fear of missing out on something by being one place when I should have been in the other.

One thing keeping me in the Bay Area was the "community cultural center" (that was how we'd sold it to the zoning board, anyway) I was helping to organize and build on Gilman Street in West Berkeley. It was basically a warehouse where we planned to put on punk rock shows, but with the help, inspiration, and major financial contributions of *Maximum Rocknroll*'s Tim Yohannan, we thought we could make it something more than just another music venue.

The theory was that in a space where people were free to interact and create without outside interference, great things could and would happen. It wasn't that far removed from the romantic ideal that had brought me to Spy Rock.

I used the rest of my harvest time income for two new solar panels, doubling my system's output. Now the Lookouts could practice long into the night without running down the batteries, and I could brag—to this day I have no way of knowing if it was true—that we were the world's first solar-powered band. In October we went down to Oakland to record what would become our first album.

It was way too soon. We could have used another year of practice, and we were so nervous about being in a "real" recording studio that we played everything at double speed, obliterating any traces of melody or lyrical and rhythmic subtleties that might once have existed.

There's a punk rock philosophy that claims anybody can be in a band. It doesn't follow that everyone should be. Let alone that they should immediately put out a record. Oblivious, we plowed ahead anyway. The album remains, even to this day, a bit of an embarrassment, but it was something to build on, a foundation of belief in ourselves that flew in the face of the ridicule and neglect our efforts had elicited from our fellow mountaineers.

So as 1986 wound down, there was reason for hope, maybe even a little excitement. It was a huge change from the desperation of a year before, though I felt far from secure, far from sure that my plans, hopes, and dreams would end in anything but more trouble, sorrow, and frustration. At least, I told myself, I wasn't stuck in a rut anymore. There was no longer much doubt that my work and crazy schemes were getting me somewhere. Whether it was anyplace I'd want to be remained to be seen.

seven

One of the drawbacks of dividing my time between Spy Rock and the city was the rigmarole I had to go through every time I left the mountain or returned from San Francisco.

Summertime was easy. Leave enough food for the dogs and cats, make sure the water tanks were full and the drip irrigation timers working, and I could take off, confident things would run smoothly for a week or so. I no longer even bothered locking the door. Not that I could; the lock had broken sometime in 1985, and I had no idea how to go about fixing it.

Winter was more complicated. It was crucial to drain every last drop of water from the pipes and water heater. If I slipped up—as I did on a couple occasions—I would come home to shattered pipes, a broken toilet, or a no longer functioning shower or bathtub. Sometimes I was able to repair the damage. Most of the pipes were easy to mend, and although the new toilet I installed wobbled like a ship at sea, at least it worked.

But the shower plumbing was embedded behind beautiful redwood paneling. Without taking a crowbar to the walls, I couldn't get at the broken pipes. I was able to get the tub working again, but from that winter on, showers on Spy Rock would be a thing of the past.

Some of these problems could have been avoided if, like city people, I could leave the heat on while I was away, but that isn't possible with a wood stove. Even if you had a magical robot or firewood fairy to continually fill the stove, there was always the possibility of a chimney fire—easy enough to deal with if you're on the premises, but capable of consuming the entire house if you're not.

Earthquakes, too, were a danger. I'd already been through one that was strong enough to throw me out of bed and onto the floor, where I lay for what felt like a very long minute watching the rafters sway and wondering if the roof was about to cave in on me. That particular quake leveled some bridges farther to the north on Highway 101, but thankfully the stove and water heater weren't torn loose from their moorings. A couple more notches up the Richter scale and I might not have been so lucky.

Among the unhappiest consequences of not living on the mountain fulltime was that the house itself went into a slow but inexorable decline. Most of the wooden awnings eventually collapsed under the weight of accumulated snow. The siding on the wall that faced out over the valley buckled and came loose after I unthinkingly cut down the stately old oak that had shielded it from the sun and wind.

Looking for more light and a better view, I'd had no idea what havoc unbroken sunlight could wreak, even on redwood, one of nature's most weather-resistant materials. Anne might have known how to fix or replace the cracked and broken boards, but I'd never even mastered the art of hammering in nails without destroying my thumb and anything else in the immediate vicinity.

The sensible thing would have been to hire a professional to repair the damages to the house, but that was easier said than done. The marijuana trade had hopelessly skewed the local economy. Carpenters, electricians, and plumbers were in constant demand, but they could earn so much more from marijuana, whether growing it themselves or doing construction for the big time growers, that it was almost impossible to hire them for "normal" jobs.

I finally found one guy who started painting and repairing my siding, but he disappeared after three days, never to be seen or heard from again. A neighbor told me he'd been offered five grand to put in a shed for an indoor grower down on the Lower Loop.

Being away as much as I was, it was easy not to notice— or to semi-deliberately ignore—how badly the house was deteriorating. The Gilman Street Project, which I'd been working on for the past six months, opened its doors at the end of 1986, and was hosting two or three shows every weekend. It was by far the best place the Lookouts had ever played, and regardless of who was on stage, Gilman was becoming the center of the punk rock universe. Staying home to tend the farm paled by comparison.

I bought my first computer, a primitive Macintosh. Its 512-kilobyte memory wouldn't have been able to power a cell phone a decade later, but in 1987 it offered a dazzling new technology that I struggled to master. When, after 12 hours of false starts and confusion, I formatted and printed a paragraph of text—something I could have done in two minutes on my typewriter—I felt like Neil Armstrong taking his first step on the moon.

The ability to manipulate fonts and type sizes let me fit much more content into *Lookout* magazine. Around the same time I found a copy shop in Berkeley where I could print the *Lookout* for half what I'd been paying.

The deal was to get better still. One day the manager pulled me aside and said, "Yo, I been reading that paper of yours. You got some funny-ass shit in there." He then offered me a super-discounted price—I doubt it even covered his costs—and the *Lookout*'s print run shot further up into the thousands.

It felt like I was on a roll. Redoubling my efforts to cover everything of interest in the Bay Area as well as the Emerald Triangle, I also seemed—finally—to be gaining some grudging acceptance from Mendocino County readers.

I still had enemies, of course, and even people who agreed with me sometimes cringed at my more purplish invective. But agree or not, they were engaging with me. It got to where I could have filled entire issues of the *Lookout* with nothing but readers' letters and my long-winded responses.

While you could digest the *Laytonville Ledger* in five or ten minutes, the *Lookout* kept people entertained and/or infuriated for hours. Even those who claimed they never read "that rag" had opinions about it. Unwilling to furnish me with more fodder for my letters section, they'd write to the *Ledger* to complain about my latest outrages.

The *Ledger* had pointedly ignored me for the past couple of years, but it was hard to do so now that I was generating so much controversy. When Laytonville was thrown into an uproar by Sheila Larson's attempt to build an asphalt plant in the center of town, it became impossible.

Sheila owned Boomer's Bar, for many years the town's only saloon. A new, more hippie-oriented place called the Crossroads had recently opened across the street, but if you were looking for the real Laytonville, you had to poke your head into Boomer's, where cowboys, Indians, loggers, and a sprinkling of brave or inebriated hippies whiled away the hours in fragile harmony.

Boomer's was set on a large piece of Highway 101 frontage, near the intersection with Branscomb Road. If Laytonville could be said to have a heart, this was it: Geiger's General Store on one corner, the high school just down the block. The bank, post office, and liquor store were a few minutes' stroll away. It was the only place for miles around where you could park your truck and take care of most of your errands on foot. And it was here that Sheila thought she'd put her factory.

Certain old-timers—the Geigers, the Harwoods, who owned the lumber mill, the logging supplies magnate Bill Bailey—were accustomed to having things done their way without a question or an eyebrow being raised. That's not to say they ran roughshod over the town. On the contrary, they were left unchallenged not only because of their money and influence, but also because they were generally perceived as having the community's best interests at heart.

Sheila Larson had been around a while, but had not achieved—and probably never would—the landed gentry status she assumed she had. Her misperception led to a greater error: thinking everyone—or at least everyone who mattered—would agree that what was good for Sheila's business was good for Laytonville. Touting the jobs and income it would supposedly produce, she announced her asphalt plant not as a proposal but a *fait accompli*.

Given the way business had traditionally been conducted in Laytonville, she probably never dreamed anyone apart from the usual handful of nitpickers and naysayers would find fault with the noise, pollution, and nearly nonstop truck traffic the plant would produce. This proved to be a serious miscalculation on her part.

But no one, myself included, could have predicted the upwelling of protest that saw half the town descend on the public hearing where the asphalt plant's fate would be decided. In a special edition of the *Lookout* thrown together that night and in circulation the following morning, I described the crowd as something straight out of Frank Capra and Norman Rockwell: "Country bumpkins, urban expatriates, leather-skinned pioneer women, brown-rice-and-tofu hippies, sweet-faced grandmothers, and good old boys who self-consciously doffed their NRA caps as they entered the room."

Journalistically I felt it was my finest hour. Not only had I covered and published a breaking story before the *Ledger* noticed it was happening, I'd also helped provide a focal point for the opposition. In a stunning reversal, the county stopped Sheila's project in its tracks, and my social status was elevated—in some eyes, at least—from persona non grata to The Man Who Helped Save Laytonville.

As I made my usual rounds around town, people stopped to shake my hand and thank me. If Laytonville had been an actual city rather than an unincorporated wide spot in the road, I might have harbored delusions about running for mayor.

I was blindsided by the backlash that followed. When, later that week, the *Ledger* published its first-ever editorial, I was surprised to find it was not about the asphalt plant controversy, but about me. The verdict was not complimentary.

Nor were the several pages of letters from indignant citizens. Agree or disagree with Sheila Larson, what really had them up in arms was the way I'd characterized the town and its people.

"If he doesn't like it here, why doesn't he leave?" and "Who appointed this Livermore guy to speak for me?" were among the more moderate sentiments. "I wouldn't vote for Livermore if he were running for septic tank inspector," said a slightly more vexed resident, "even though the job does suit him." Another, perhaps channeling Spiro Agnew, denounced me as a "jabbering jackal" and a "pompous, presumptuous, pretentious pedant."

That contribution, titled "Every Town Needs A Village Idiot," prompted one of my few defenders to fire back,

"Laytonville doesn't need a village idiot, it is one." But even he called my account of the hearing "largely factual, but unkind."

"[Laytonville's] dusty roads, gun-racked pickups and wild-eyed dope growers make it an easy target for ridicule," I'd written, before adding, "While it's not cute or quaint or glamorous, there are those who happily call it home, and even those who, inexplicable as it may seem, love the place."

That was my point: I, against all expectations, had become one of those people. I thought I'd been penning a love letter to the town I had finally begun to think of as my home. The response I'd gotten was to be told, in loud and certain terms, that the feeling wasn't mutual.

I lay low for a couple weeks, waiting for things to settle down. They didn't. When I finally ventured out, it was not into town, but to the Mad Creek Inn, a roadhouse 14 miles north of town that dated back to the 1920s. In its heyday it had hosted the likes of Clark Gable and Carole Lombard.

Its current owner, widely and affectionately known as Mad Mary, had transformed the restaurant into an almost magical place, a relaxed candlelit refuge from the workaday realities of mountain life. For a couple of years I'd been stopping in every week or two to play the piano.

My repertoire—a mélange of show tunes, 60s and 70s folk and pop hits, and my own New Age improvisational noodling—was slim, but sufficient to earn me a free meal, a few dollars in tips, and appreciation from most of the customers. Few if any of them were aware I was the notorious Lawrence Livermore.

Until, that is, I flippantly mentioned in the *Lookout* that my arch-nemesis Bill Bailey had dropped a $20 bill—the biggest single tip I'd ever received—in my basket. Despite all the ink I'd spilled on branding the logging supplies baron as a single-minded ogre, I was genuinely touched by his generosity, and thought readers should know about it.

The net result, though, was that I had outed myself as the mysterious Mad Creek pianist, and Mary was furious.

"How could you?" she seethed, her normally blissful face roiling like a late-summer thundercloud. If she wanted to maintain the tranquil atmosphere in which her business flourished, she couldn't be seen giving aid and comfort to someone who routinely had half the town chewing on barbed wire and spitting nails.

My piano-playing days were at an end, and so were Mary's wonderful home-cooked meals. Angry and hurt, I retreated to my Spy Rock sanctuary, feeling more isolated than ever. What else could go wrong? Plenty, it turned out.

Indiana Slim, one of the only local musicians who'd ever shown any interest in us, asked if the Lookouts would play at a benefit show his band was organizing for the family of a young girl who'd fallen into a rain-swollen creek and drowned. He suggested, and I agreed, that it could be an opportunity to mend fences with the community. I'm not sure what, or if, Slim was thinking, but in retrospect, I must have been nuts.

Even without the recent unpleasantness, the Lookouts would hardly be a welcome addition to the lineup. Our raucous, aggressive style of music would be especially inappropriate at a family-oriented affair with a sad and somber purpose. And at least half the audience would consist of people who'd recently been calling for my head to be hung from the nearest lamppost.

None of this occurred to me, though; the only thing I worried about was Piano Jimmy, sworn enemy and bane of the Lookouts' existence, and a featured member of Slim's band. "Will Jimmy be all right with this?" I asked. Slim said not to worry. He'd take care of Jimmy.

Perhaps it slipped his mind. Or, more likely, he decided not to bother mentioning it to Jimmy, relying instead on good intentions and the spirit of rock and roll to smooth over any difficulties.

A large, enthusiastic crowd watched and danced to Slim's band. By the time they were done, it was getting late. Some people, especially those who'd brought kids, were drifting toward the exits.

The Lookouts dragged our equipment to the stage and started setting up. Ignoring us, Piano Jimmy and a couple of his friends began noodling and riffing on one of the blues-based boogies they specialized in.

"We're supposed to play now," I said. "Slim invited us." Jimmy responded with a smirk and continued plinking away at his piano.

I lost it. Jumping on stage, I pounded on Jimmy's keyboard, busting up whatever melody he might have been playing.

You don't do that to a musician, not even a genial, good-tempered one. Barely missing a beat, he hit me full on in the face with one of his hamhock-sized fists. The "fight," if you could call it that, was over before it began. The closest thing to a victory I could claim was managing to stay on my feet when I should have been flat on my back.

Jimmy's impromptu jam session meandered on for another hour until the hall was nearly empty. The Lookouts were then given a chance to play for the handful of diehards that remained. It didn't take us long to send them on their way.

It wasn't until I got home that night that I realized I was wearing the most spectacular black eye of my life (as you'd imagine, given my penchant for shooting my mouth off, there had been others). Normally I would have shrugged it off, but the following day was our record release show at Gilman.

I wasn't looking forward to the questions and ridicule that were sure to ensue, but Kain and Tre helped defuse the issue by using a magic marker to draw black eyes on themselves. Members of the audience followed suit, turning my embarrassment into a funny sort of triumph.

That same month I began writing a monthly column ("Lookout! It's Lawrence Livermore!") for *Maximum Rocknroll*. My column header featured a photo of me that had originally appeared in a Mendocino County magazine called the *New Settler Interview*. Someone at *MRR* doctored the photo, adding a cartoonish black eye that would become an integral part of my public image for some time to come.

While the Gilman show turned out great, the record itself was neither as good nor as successful as I'd hoped. Friends and fans bought the first couple hundred copies, but the remaining 800 would sit in my kitchen for the next year. I was disappointed, but had no time to sit around moping. Another uproar had erupted in Laytonville, and again I was at the center of it.

Trying to get even with the *Ledger* for the attacks it had unleashed on me, I used my newly learned computer skills to create a mashup of its logo with that of the *Lookout*. Calling my next issue *The Laytonville Lookout and Ledger*, I claimed to have successfully sued the *Ledger* for libel, taken over its ownership and merged it with the *Lookout*.

Ridiculous? Of course, but there were people who took it seriously. Even those who didn't were none too happy with my front-page picture of Jesus on the cross entitled, "Easter 1987: [*Ledger* editor] John Weed, Sheila Larson, and Piano Jimmy party at Lawrence Livermore's crucifixion on Cahto Mountain." Laytonville was not a deeply religious community, but it was religious enough to take offense at that.

Or, I should say, parts of Laytonville were. When I tentatively ventured into town again, something seemed to have shifted. There were dirty looks a-plenty, as per usual, but they began to be matched, maybe even outnumbered, by thumbs-up and knowing smiles. If I'd accepted every free drink I was offered at the Crossroads that afternoon, I'd have been too drunk to walk home, let alone drive.

After years of feeling like Public Enemy Number One, it was hugely satisfying to feel that some locals were coming to like, appreciate, or at least tolerate me. I might not have been the most popular guy in town, but at last I was beginning to feel as though I truly belonged here. And not just in my private fiefdom atop Iron Peak, but in the community as a whole. It was an entirely new experience.

I had never before lived where it was possible to know most of my neighbors, let alone get along with them. Letting go of the alienation that had always been my default setting, I was able for the first time to commit to a place and its people, to unabashedly admit that, with all its failings and frustrations, this was my home, and I loved it.

My new sense of belongingness wasn't enough to stop me from feeling lonely a great deal of the time. More than two years after Anne had left, I still hadn't been involved in anything that would qualify as a date, let alone a relationship. I thought things might be changing when I met a beautiful young woman in San Francisco, and change they did, but not in the direction I'd hoped for.

Long before we met in person, I'd seen her in a photo taken at a 1986 Lookouts show in Golden Gate Park. I spent several months asking if anyone knew her before discovering she was a fellow contributor to *MRR* and a volunteer at Gilman Street.

Friendly, outgoing, and always ready for a good conversation, she made it clear from the start that her romantic interest in me was slightly less than zilch. I treasured the long, heartfelt talks we shared; it didn't dawn on to me until long afterward that they consisted mostly of her explaining a) why I was wrong about almost everything; and b) how ludicrous it was to imagine she could ever be attracted to me.

Somehow that didn't discourage me. I invited her up to Spy Rock, and though I never figured out why, she accepted. She loved the mountain, though I couldn't help getting the impression she'd have enjoyed it even more if I hadn't been there.

Still, we got along well for most of the weekend, and it was a pleasant change to spend time with someone who seemed to revel as much as I did in the wonder of a Spy Rock spring. On Sunday, just before driving back to the city, we walked up the road to a rock formation that looked as though it had been lifted from one of those Chinese misty mountain scrolls.

Ruf-Ruf ran ahead, covering 10 or 20 steps for each of ours, charging into the bushes in search of grouse, wood rats, squirrels, or anything else that might be fun to kill. Suddenly she reared up on her hind legs and gave a sharp yelp.

I thought I saw something moving in the grass, but before I had time to wonder what it could be, I heard a chilling rattle. I assumed, reasonably enough, that Ruf-Ruf had scared up a snake, but by the time I got there, it had vanished. Ruf-Ruf looked unscathed, if a little spooked by her close call.

As lively as ever, she followed us back to the house, giving us a tail-wagging farewell as we left for San Francisco. When I got back two days later, I was surprised not to find her waiting for me in her usual spot at the top of the driveway. As I approached the house, I saw her swaying feebly, trying as hard as she could to stay on her feet, but looking as though the slightest breeze might send her toppling to the ground.

She'd lost half her body weight; hollowed-out flesh hung down in folds from her stomach. This time I had no trouble locating the puncture wounds left by the rattlesnake. She'd been bitten in the middle of her throat. It was a miracle she'd survived this long.

I tried to give her some milk, then some water, but she could hardly move her head, or even her tongue. I got a few drops into her mouth, but she was too weak to swallow. I carried her into the house, begging her not to give up, but in my heart I was pretty certain she was going to die.

Unable to think of anything else I could do, I tried to lift her spirits by singing to her. Sitting at the piano, I racked my brain for an appropriate song before hitting upon a childhood favorite of mine, "How Much Is That Doggie In The Window?"

I sang it over and over, tears streaming down my cheeks, watching for any sign that she might be perking up. If nothing else, I thought, my mawkish caterwauling might inspire a desperate attempt to drag herself out of earshot.

What happened instead was like a movie—a B-grade, soppy potboiler awash in schmaltzy sentiment, perhaps, but a movie nonetheless. My tinkling piano seemed to be joined by a swelling string section as Ruf-Ruf tilted her head ever so slightly. Her face took on that quizzical look with which she'd always observed her master's strange behavior.

Her eyes opened a bit wider, her head seeming to nod almost imperceptibly in time with the music. She lapped weakly at the saucer of milk I'd left in front of her. A few minutes later she finished it and begged silently for more.

It would be a couple of days before she could eat solid food, and several more until she was strong enough to wander around again on her own, but the crisis had passed. Some nerve damage remained, leaving her with a slight palsy that she never completely shook off, but otherwise she made a full recovery.

Ruf-Ruf's close call left me feeling guiltier than ever about spending so much time away from the mountain. But it was hard sticking close to home when so much was happening elsewhere. The Lookouts were getting asked to play gigs up and down the coast, and Gilman Street was not just thriving, it was producing a crop of young new bands as exciting as anything I'd heard since, well, ever.

I'd begun renting a room in an apartment situated midway between the Mission and the Castro in San Francisco, sometimes spending as many as three or four nights a week there. It was home to Dave Dictor, singer for multi-acronymed band MDC ("Millions of Dead Cops," "Multi-Death Corporation," "Millions of Damn Christians"), and to a fellow Gilman volunteer named David Hayes.

Our place became known as "The Rathouse," thanks to David's pet rat and the general punkish disreputability in which we dwelt. Along with our fourth housemate, a Three Stooges-loving Brooklyn expat named Joe Britz, we published a zine called *Tales From The Rathouse*, and played host to a revolving cast of misfits, exiles, and troublemakers.

Our most memorable exploit unfolded when Pope John Paul II visited Mission Dolores, located directly across the street. The Secret Service, who'd been charged with guarding the Pope, paid everyone in the neighborhood a visit in advance, warning us to stay off our roofs and to avoid so much as looking out, let alone opening any windows that faced the church. Having solemnly agreed to this, we surreptitiously hauled MDC's equipment to the top of the stairs just before the Pope's arrival.

When our spotter signaled that the Popemobile had turned into Dolores Street, we dragged the amps and drums onto the roof in time for the band to serenade His Holiness (and the neighborhood for several blocks around) with a couple minutes of "This Blood's For You," one of their more scabrous anti-religious epics. Then the Secret Service descended en masse, confiscated the band equipment, and took down all our names as potential terror suspects.

From time to time, David Hayes and I talked about starting some sort of record label to document the scene emerging at Gilman Street. David had already put together a cassette compilation of local bands, and been asked by *Maximum Rocknroll* to produce a double 7" EP sampler called *Turn It Around*, meant to both showcase and benefit Gilman.

One of the most talked-about bands was Operation Ivy, who played a blend of ska and punk that felt equally inspired by the Specials and the Clash, but somehow managed to transcend both of them. They'd been together all of three months, but, at least within the incestuous little goldfish bowl of Gilman Street, had become instant superstars.

When I first saw them, in September of 1987, I'd never heard an Operation Ivy song, didn't have the slightest idea what the words were, yet within seconds I was singing along as if I'd known them all my life. Me and everybody else in the room. So many audience members jumped on stage to join in the opening chorus of "Sleep Long" that the band totally disappeared from view.

It was one of the most amazing performances I'd ever seen. I was catching my breath on the sidewalk out front when their guitarist, a skinny kid I'd always known as Tim but who'd recently changed his name to Lint, came bouncing up to me.

"Yo Larry, did you like our band?" I never fully understood

why I replied the way I did. I intended to say something along the lines of, "Yeah, that was really good." What came out was, "Do you want to make a record?"

Just like that, I was in the record business. Operation Ivy were surprised (years later they admitted that they'd thought I was crazy), but unhesitatingly said yes. Having "signed" my first band, I turned around and asked Isocracy, Gilman's other in-house favorite, if they wanted to do a 7" as well.

When I had a quiet moment to think about it, I realized I was probably in way over my head. Luckily, David Hayes, who was hoping to put out an EP for Corrupted Morals, agreed to join forces with me, bringing his much-needed graphic design and organizational skills to the project.

Extensive discussion ensued about what to call our new company. David, an avid bicyclist, liked the name Sprocket Records. I argued for Lookout, on grounds of existing name recognition, and either my powers of persuasion or sheer persistence carried the day. David shepherded the bands in and out of Oakland's Dangerous Rhythm studio, where, working with an up-and-coming independent producer named Kevin Army, they turned out their respective tracks in a matter of hours.

At the last minute, I impulsively (this seemed to be how I was doing everything) asked Crimpshrine, another Berkeley band, if they'd like us to release their 7" as well. We took out an ad in *Maximum Rocknroll* ("Nobody buys 7" records anymore, so we're putting out four of them"), and Lookout Records was born.

All the while, I was still pining pointlessly after the same woman who'd spent the past year evading or ignoring my advances. Just before winter set in she paid another visit to Spy Rock. I took her to the Harvest Ball at Beginnings, a redwood hobbit hall and community center tucked away in the woods of Southern Humboldt, where she danced with everyone in the room but me.

I suspected her of doing it deliberately, as a way of making sure I knew where I stood. For some reason it didn't bother me as much as it once would have. Maybe the change of season combined with new adventures looming on the horizon eased my wounded feelings.

It was gratifying to see her appreciating and embracing our local culture, especially after I'd endured so many of her snide remarks about my "hippie" values. I'd repeatedly tried and failed to convince her there was something powerfully authentic, almost elemental, about this way of life I had embraced. Revolving around the rhythms of the earth and its seasons, I argued, it didn't differ so much from the indigenous agricultural societies she idealized.

She'd sneered at that notion, yet here she was, twirling like a native in the dreamy half-light of a timeless celebration of the land and its bounty. My hippie friends thought she was wonderful, and I barely had the heart to tell them she was actually one of those nihilistic urban punk rockers who mystified and even frightened them.

It had long been one of my goals to bridge the gap between the countercultures, to convince punks and hippies they had more in common than they thought. At last I dared to believe I might be making some progress. On the long, late-night drive back to Spy Rock, her tacit acknowledgment that there was more than she'd imagined to this strange backwoods realm I inhabited was met by my quiet acceptance that she was never going to love me.

The mild weather lingered late that year, almost into December. I should have known better, but I let it seduce me into greeting winter's arrival largely unprepared. I was spending a longer than usual weekend in the Bay Area when Spy Rock was left buried under a foot of snow that, followed by a hard freezing rain, left the roads hopelessly impassable.

I would have liked to forget about the mountain until spring, or at least until the worst of the snow and ice had melted, but I couldn't. It would be only a matter of days before my dogs and cats would be out of food. Like it or not, I was going to have to go in on foot to re-supply them.

The county had cleared the first few miles of Spy Rock Road, but at the turnoff to Iron Peak I had to abandon my truck and travel the remaining four miles on snowshoes. It would be a thousand-foot climb up to the ridge, followed by a similar descent on the other side.

The afternoon was well underway when I started walking, and the darkening, lowering skies made it look even later. I made good time, though, even with 50 pounds of dog food on my back. Arriving at my house shortly after 4 pm, I refilled the animals' food trays, petted and played with them a while, then went inside for a brief rest before starting my trip back.

The windows rattled and a chilly draft went whistling through the house. A storm was blowing in, a bad one from the sound of it. Lying on the sofa by the fire, I tried to keep my eyes open, aware that the longer I waited, the likelier it was that I'd have to battle my way out through a blizzard.

I desperately wanted to sleep, but if the weather forecast was right, by morning the snow level would have dropped dramatically, my truck would be buried under a couple feet of snow, and I'd be stranded on the mountain for the duration. Which at that time of year could be weeks or months.

Even then I might have considered sticking around if I'd had an adequate supply of firewood and food, but I had only a little of the former and none of the latter. As darkness fell, I hoped against hope that the snow would hold off until later that night, but when I opened the door to leave, it was already falling hard, driven at a sharp angle by the quickening wind.

Worried about feral dogs or other wild animals, I brought along my shotgun just in case. Striding along in my long trench coat, weapon strapped across my shoulder, I felt like a Russian soldier fleeing Napoleon or the Nazis across the Eastern Front. Before I'd made it halfway up the first small hill my legs had turned to jelly.

I could manage about 10 steps before having to stop and rest. Normally the hike out would take an hour and a half; having to fight my way into the wind and snow might add another hour. But at the rate I was moving, it would take me most of the night. If I made it at all.

I wasn't sure I would. An eight mile round trip, even on snowshoes, wouldn't normally be a big deal, but hauling that 50 pounds of dog food had taken more out of me than I'd expected. Making things worse, the first three miles of the trip out were a continuous uphill climb.

I toyed with the idea of turning back, but with no food in the house and no idea of when I'd be able to get out again, it made no sense. An equally frightening possibility was that even if I made it to my truck, it might already have been snowed in, leaving me stranded on the side of the mountain, miles from both home and highway.

None of my choices looked promising; I could only try to pick the one least likely to lead to disaster. At 9 pm, almost four hours after starting out, I still had a mile—the steepest mile—to go before I'd reach the ridge and be able to start my descent.

Sheer force of will enabled me to up my pace from 10 steps at a time to 30, but I still had to follow each burst of walking with several minutes of rest. As I dragged myself up the north face of Iron Peak, I gained one small advantage: the ridge and mountain combined to shield me from the worst of the wind.

That same wind nearly sent me tumbling back down the way I'd come when, around 10 pm, I crested the ridge top. I shouted with exhilaration, knowing the final mile would all be downhill, but heard nothing. Either I'd lost my voice or the sound had been swept away by the storm before it could reach my ears.

It would be easy from now on, I kept telling myself. Even the weather seemed to cooperate: once I left the ridge and headed down Iron Peak Road, the wind subsided and the stinging icy pellets that had been ripping at my face turned to great fluffy flakes, prettier to look at and far easier to walk through. The only downside to this kind of snow was that it was piling up much faster on the ground.

Desperate to reach my truck while it was still possible to drive out, I stopped taking rest periods and charged straight ahead. At last I saw it, dimly silhouetted, emerging from the darkness, almost as if it were a mirage, no more, perhaps, than three or four hundred yards ahead.

I felt like I must be entering a semi-hallucinatory state, because it looked as though I could practically reach out and touch the truck, feel the warmth, safety, and deliverance it promised. Quietly congratulating myself at having survived this journey, I steeled myself for the final push.

I almost made it.

I don't know exactly how it happened. I think my snowshoes must have gotten tangled up with each other. The next thing I knew I was face down in a snowdrift, barely able to move. I couldn't get my snowshoes separated, and somehow the shotgun had gotten stuck in there, too. Eventually I managed to turn so I was looking up instead of down, but the lower half of me remained hopelessly immobile.

A sinking feeling told me this was as far as I'd be going. Already the snow was beginning to cover me. And I was tired. So very tired. I'd read stories about people freezing to death, stories that sounded much like this. I struggled a bit more, but most of my muscles had gone numb. I stopped fighting, and felt the snowdrift turn into a deliciously luxurious featherbed. I could happily have lain there forever.

At the same time, I knew that if I stayed there much longer, I was going to die, that the process of my body shutting down might already be underway. I felt a great sadness, not so much because I was afraid of dying, but because I'd left so many things undone, so many hopes unrealized.

Those records we'd recorded would come out without me—David would take care of that—and a neighbor might stop by before my dogs and cats ran out of food, but as for me, it would be days—at least—before anyone would travel down that road and find me lying frozen and half buried in the snow.

Ah well, I sighed, nothing to be done about it now. I wished it could have ended differently, a little less ignominiously, but we're not always given that choice. I marveled at the soft beauty of the night, at the bitter irony of it all, at the way millions of snowflakes floated toward me, displaying the same effortless grace with which the firmament of stars had danced above me on long-ago summer nights. Whispering a bittersweet goodbye to all that had been, that could and should and would have been, I closed my eyes and slept.

eight

I don't know how much time passed. Maybe half an hour; maybe only a few minutes. My mind had lapsed into a dreamlike state, but it was a dream where nothing happened. In my Catholic school days, the nuns had taught us about limbo, a neutral nether realm to which God consigned innocent but unbaptized infants.

Neither heaven nor hell, neither good nor bad, devoid of meaning or purpose: it was exactly the sort of place I found myself in now. Everything was swathed in a serene, mysterious gray, as if I were caught in one of those low-hanging clouds that periodically enveloped Iron Peak, only without the chilly dampness. Instead I felt embraced by warm, welcoming arms that I couldn't imagine ever wanting to tear myself away from.

Yet something nagged at me, tugged at my mind, insisted I pay attention. Against my will, my eyes snapped open. I shut them and tried to slip back into that gentle cloud of oblivion, but they refused to stay closed. Now I was angry. I could feel the cold again, could feel snowflakes batting at my face like icy butterflies.

Tossing my head from side to side to avoid them, I caught sight of my truck a few hundred yards down the road. I'd been trying to get there, hadn't I? Why? I vaguely remembered a time when it had seemed important.

Suddenly I was overcome by a moment of clarity. I was on a mission. If I didn't make it to the truck, something terrible would happen. What it was, and what I was supposed to do about it, I didn't know, but thought I'd better try to find out. Realizing I couldn't stand up, let alone walk, I hit upon the idea of swimming.

If you could have watched me from above, you would have assumed I'd gone mad. It would have looked as though, lying on the side of a mountain in the midst of a blizzard, I was trying to make snow angels. If you'd asked me, however, I would have told you I was doing the breast stroke.

It got me nowhere, but when I switched to a modified dog paddle, I found myself moving forward. I don't know if I pulled myself all the way to the truck like that. My first untrammeled memory is of opening the truck door, so by that time I must have made it onto my feet.

I was too weak to lift myself into the cab, but by leaning back onto the driver's seat and grabbing hold of the armrest on the passenger side, I was able to pull myself in. Once behind the wheel, I still couldn't muster the strength to lift my legs, and finally resorted to picking them up with my hands, one at a time, as if they were a couple pieces of cordwood.

The engine started easily enough, but my legs were so numb I couldn't operate the brake or accelerator pedals. I sat there flummoxed by this dilemma until the warmth from the heater breathed a little life into my muscles.

Parked on a steep hill as I was, I barely needed to step on the gas. In fact, the tiniest bit of over-acceleration would send me careening over the cliff, as would hitting the brakes too hard or suddenly.

My biggest problem would be getting the truck turned around and headed downhill again. I'd left it facing uphill, in a spot where the road was so narrow that reversing direction would have been tough under normal conditions. Now it was next to impossible to tell how deep the snow was or, more importantly, where exactly the road ended and the cliff began.

In the end, all it took was time and patience. I put the transmission in gear while pressing lightly on the brake, backed and filled 15 or 20 times, and was on my way. There were spots where I almost got stuck in snow that had drifted across the road, but after what I'd been through, nothing was going to stop me.

Most of the way, I just let the truck roll, never fully taking my foot off the brake so as not to pick up too much speed. There was snow even at the lower altitudes, which was unusual, though not unheard of. Navigating Spy Rock Road was like steering my way down five miles of a fiendishly loopy toboggan run. Snow was still falling when I finally reached the pavement, but by then only a little of it was sticking.

At 2 am I pounded on the door of the Cottage Motel in downtown Laytonville and convinced the none-too-pleased manager to rent me one of the old cabins out back. I slept for the next day and a half. By Sunday afternoon I was ready to continue my journey south, but every muscle I owned ached so miserably that I gave up on the idea and went back to bed until Monday.

By the time I made it back to the Bay Area, more than three days after setting out on this not so great adventure, the time was already drawing near when I'd have to make another trip up the mountain. Luckily the weather eased up soon afterward, and for the rest of the winter, I was able to drive in and out without too many problems.

"I hope you appreciate me risking my life for you," I made a point of telling the dogs and cats the next several times I saw them. They responded, as usual, by climbing all over me when I arrived and staring with blank bemusement as I departed again.

In mid-January, David Hayes and I set up a table at the back of Gilman Street and put Lookout Records' first four 7" releases on sale. I was amazed at how much excitement they generated, considering how reluctant punks are to show enthusiasm about anything, especially things they actually like.

I'd been hoping to sell a couple hundred copies of each release, which was how it had worked with the Lookouts LP. In that case, we—I should say "I," since I was the one who'd put up the cash for this operation—wouldn't lose too much money. My definition of success going into the project had been to break even; the idea of making even a small profit existed only in my wildest dreams.

What happened instead was that we sold out of records within a month and pressed a thousand more copies of each. That was when Ruth Schwartz, who'd used her profits from releasing the first Faith No More album to set up an independent distribution company called Mordam Records, asked if she could take us on as a client.

Mordam had a lot of clout, not least because they handled the then-very-much-in-demand Dead Kennedys catalog. They were also, unlike many distributors, scrupulously honest. This meant that we not only sold far more records, but also that we got paid for them like clockwork, every month. Even the pile of unsold Lookouts albums finally disappeared from my kitchen.

In February I got a letter from some college students in Arcata, asking me to bring some Lookout bands up to play a show. Arcata, although it lay at the northern end of the Emerald Triangle, was not a place I knew well. I'd stopped there once on a road trip; stepping out of my car, I was immediately greeted by the sound of an ancient Led Zeppelin tune echoing through deserted streets. Convinced the place was haunted by the ghosts of undead hippies, I hadn't gone back.

I was more familiar with Eureka, Arcata's larger, but mostly forlorn and unlovely counterpart that lurked and slouched beneath foul-smelling clouds of pulp mill smoke across the bay. In the 19th century Eureka had been a boomtown that had grown rich cutting and milling the redwood logs that built San Francisco, but the ensuing century hadn't treated it so well.

The once elegant Victorian homes and mansions that lined its streets looked disheveled and dilapidated; its ornate and opulent Old Town had degenerated into a shabby, dispirited Skid Row. I liked the place for its near-poetic levels of bleakness and despair, but had never felt inclined to spend a great deal of time there.

Arcata, on the other hand, was home to Humboldt State University, the North Coast's only four-year college. Despite sitting for much of the year beneath the semi-perpetual fog bank that shrouded the shoreline all the way up to Oregon, the town had a palpably sunnier, more upbeat disposition than Eureka. Young people from across the Emerald Triangle gravitated there, even if they weren't studying at HSU, in search of the semi-urban culture and excitement that simply wasn't on offer in their hometowns.

Even taking this into account, I was astounded at the size of the crowd that turned out for our show. People had traveled upwards of a hundred miles to see Operation Ivy, the Lookouts, Isocracy, Crimpshrine, and Arcata's own Schmidtheads. It was the best show we'd played up to that time, both musically and in terms of what it represented.

Over the past year and a half Gilman Street had played host to any number of epochally memorable shows, to the point where I was telling people that we were entering a new golden age of Bay Area music. More than two decades had passed since the heyday of the 1960s Haight-Ashbury scene that had briefly turned San Francisco into a musical and cultural touchstone for much of the planet, but the city still clung—with unbecoming tenacity, I thought—to what little remained of that faded glory.

I hadn't made it to San Francisco until the tail end of the 60s, but I'd been to the Fillmore, been to the Avalon and the Straight Theater, and what I was seeing at Gilman was imbued—albeit on a smaller scale—with the same magic, with the same sense that we were making history, creating something that at that particular moment could be found nowhere else in the world.

The Arcata show was an attempt to see if, or how well, that magic traveled. Punk, at least in my opinion, had stagnated, perhaps to the point of entering a death spiral, back in the early 80s. Obsessed with cartoonish imagery, gratuitous violence, and gutter bravado, it had extinguished nearly every spark of creativity and joy in favor of a mind-numbing and predictable conformity.

For me, Gilman and the bands that had sprung up around it represented the antidote. The music and lifestyle might have remained rooted in traditional punk, but the grim replication of pointless rituals had been replaced by an upwelling of joy and spontaneous creativity so different from what had gone before that many old-timers railed derisively against this new spirit, dismissing it as one exasperated East Coast hardcore singer did, as "Punk Rock Romper Room."

I had wondered how we'd be received by the Arcata punks, if they would find us too happy or silly, too insufficiently nihilistic, but I needn't have worried. Before the first band was finished playing, the room was filled with the same smiling faces, the same uproarious exuberance that I'd come to cherish at Gilman Street. The records we'd put out had been like a message in a bottle tossed onto a vast, uncertain sea, but here, at least, it was clear they'd landed on a friendly shore.

Still glowing with satisfaction as we started to drive away, I almost didn't see the young kid who came running out in front of my truck.

"Wait a minute!" he shouted. "Stop!!"

He was so out of breath that at first he had trouble getting me to understand what he wanted. His name, it eventually emerged, was Chris Appelgren, he was 14 ("almost 15"), and he wanted to tell me about a show he hosted on KMUD, the new community radio station in Garberville.

I'd heard of KMUD, but I hadn't actually *heard* it. It would eventually become a ubiquitous presence up and down the coast, but in those early days its transmitter was too remote and its signal too weak to produce anything but indecipherable static on my side of the mountain.

Chris was hoping to get copies of our records to play on his show. I didn't have any more with me—we'd sold everything we brought—but I promised to drop some off at the radio station the next time he was on the air.

The following week I drove into Garberville and located KMUD's studio and office, consisting of two ramshackle cabins overlooking a vacant lot at the far south end of town. Chris interviewed me, played songs from the records I'd brought, and simultaneously gave me a crash course in how to work the microphones, make public service announcements, and maintain the FCC logs.

By the time the show was over, I felt like an old hand in the radio game, and happily accepted Chris's invitation to come back two weeks later. Within a few weeks I'd graduated from semi-regular guest to co-host of KMUD's Saturday afternoon punk rock show, *Wild In The Streets*.

The name, borrowed from the Circle Jerks/Garland Jeffries song, seemed wildly out of place in a region where streets of any kind were few and far between. Even Garberville, whose population of 1,300 made it Southern Humboldt's major metropolis, could be crisscrossed and circumnavigated via skateboard in five or ten minutes.

But if Chris and I lacked literal streets to run wild in, we made up for it over the air, pumping out a variety and volume of punk rock that had seldom, if ever, resounded over those mountains and valleys before. We developed an on-air schtick—convincing because it wasn't entirely schtick—that involved me pompously kvetching about everything and anything while Chris played the breezy young upstart who viewed the world and all it contained with nonstop wide-eyed wonder.

We had occasional run-ins with the KMUD power structure, but for the most part they were amazingly tolerant about the F-bombs and obnoxious lyrics that slipped out over the air despite our best—if not always wholehearted—efforts to police ourselves.

Thinking we were in the clear as long as we avoided the "Seven Deadly Words" officially banned by the FCC, we played a Bangles parody called "Walk With An Erection." Local merchants, many of whom kept the radios in their shops tuned to KMUD, complained it was not an ideal choice for the middle of the afternoon on the Saturday before Christmas.

We thought maybe we'd gone too far this time and were headed for serious trouble, but though the station manager tried to keep a straight face while telling us, "Now, boys, let's try to be a little more considerate," he couldn't completely hide the smile that played across his face as he reviewed the offending lyrics.

We weren't the only KMUD staffers who thought broadcasting from behind the Redwood Curtain rendered us exempt from rules and regulations imposed by the federal government

("US Out Of Humboldt County" was a popular bumper sticker in those days). To many of us, KMUD sometimes felt more like a clandestine revolutionary outpost than the perfectly legitimate heartbeat of a community that it was becoming.

Never was this truer than during the growing season, when the station relayed information, rumors, and warnings about impending marijuana raids. The CAMP report—noting where helicopters, planes, or sheriff's vehicles had been spotted—was probably KMUD's single most-listened-to program.

We offered more mundane services as well, reporting on lost dogs, bear sightings, or someone who had a chain saw for sale or needed a ride to Eureka. Our public affairs and call-in programs also provided a platform and focal point for the various controversies and discussions that flared up from time to time.

One such brouhaha erupted when the Red Hot Chili Peppers played the Mateel Community Center clad only in four strategically placed socks. The teenagers in attendance thought it was hilarious, but a vocal minority of parents raised hell. So too when Oakland rapper Too Short came to town celebrating the glories of thug life and inspired some local farm boys to do a little gangbanging of their own in the parking lot.

The Mateel, like KMUD, was the product of volunteer labor and private donations, many of which no doubt originated in the underground agricultural sector. The beautiful, expensive, and artfully crafted woodwork that went into it prompted some to deride it as the "Taj Mateel." I preferred to call it the hippie Gilman.

It was an impressive accomplishment by any measure: a performance space and meeting hall capable of accommodating well over half the population of Garberville, which it sometimes had to do. Contentious issues, often sparked or inflamed via KMUD, gave rise to town meetings that, for all their rambunctiousness and occasional rancor, embodied the essential spirit of traditional American democracy.

At first only a handful of people at the station showed any appreciation for the music Chris and I played; I in turn seldom passed up an opportunity to ridicule the Grateful Dead and reggae-heavy programming that made up most of KMUD's musical output. But the cooperative nature of the station and the generally affable disposition of our fellow DJs soon led me to soft-pedal my snarky attitude.

Before long I could be heard enthusiastically—and without a trace of irony—reading promos or offering recommendations for programs I'd once scathingly dismissed as hippie claptrap. And the hippies did the same in return for our show. At the risk of sounding sappy or sentimental, it became an invaluable lesson in how to work together for the common good.

Garberville and Redway, its twin town two miles to the north, had barely 2,500 inhabitants between them, but the region was a hotbed—by middle-of-the-wilderness standards, anyway—of cultural and political activity. The more time I spent there, the less I cared about making the long trek down to the Bay Area.

Which was just as well, since I no longer had a home there. Earlier in 1988, *Maximum Rocknroll*'s Tim Yohannan—Chairman Tim, as we sometimes called him behind his back—had invited me to move into the massive Noe Valley apartment where he and several other unglamorously titled "shitworkers" lived and produced the monthly magazine.

"I was wondering if *Lookout* could use a San Francisco base of operations," was how he'd sold me on the idea, pointing out that I'd have access to *MRR*'s state-of-the-art computers and publishing facilities. But life at the Maxi-pad turned out very different from the way I'd pictured it.

From the start, Tim and I butted heads over almost everything. I'd anticipated dividing my time between Spy Rock and the city, as I'd been doing for a couple of years; Tim bristled and seethed if I was absent for more than a day or two.

I'd assumed that once finished with my *MRR* duties, I'd be free to tackle Lookout Records and *Lookout* magazine business; I learned that *MRR* duties never ended, at least not while Tim was awake, and he was not the type to waste much time sleeping. Any non-*MRR* work, when I was able to do it at all, wound up being accomplished in the very small hours of the morning.

The breaking point came when I stayed away for most of a week covering protests against government plans to open the North Coast to offshore oil drilling. People flooded into Fort Bragg by the thousands; public hearings the authorities had assumed would be a tiresome legal formality turned into a marathon teach-in of Woodstockian proportions.

Returning to San Francisco with what I thought would be an inspiring and informative story for *MRR* as well as my own magazine, I found Tim furious that I'd missed several days' worth of typing up scene reports and record reviews.

"But Tim," I argued, "You're always saying that *MRR* is about more than music. This is the biggest political protest in years, and it's about an issue that affects us all."

"That stuff isn't politics," he sneered. "It's a bunch of yuppies who don't want their oceanfront views spoiled."

Too flabbergasted to pursue this line of discussion, I could see my time at the Maxi-pad would be ending sooner rather than later. I can't remember if I told Tim I was leaving or he told me; it was one of those "You can't fire me, I quit" situations. Instead of looking for another place in the Bay Area, I packed my belongings into my truck and went back to Spy Rock for good.

Mad as I might have been at Tim, he had done me a favor. The next two years proved to be the happiest and most productive of all my time on the mountain. Struggles with the elements, the neighbors, with my own frustration and loneliness, had gradually faded away, and life took on an easy, almost carefree quality.

I'd spend days at a time working around the house or in my garden. The latter grew so fast and furiously that I could barely push my way through the lush vegetation to pick crops of eggplants, watermelons, chili peppers, and tomatillos, none of which I'd ever thought about growing before, but which flourished fantastically in the summer heat.

I had bumper crops of strawberries, raspberries, blueberries, and cherries, and the grapevines I'd put in years before finally began bearing fruit. A spindly half-dead plum tree came roaring back to life, and a nectarine tree, prolific as it was improbable, had sprung up unbidden from a long-abandoned compost heap.

The real star was the apple tree that, back in 1982, I had struggled to embed in an inhospitably rocky hillside. It had grown so tall that I could no longer reach its higher branches, but I was still able to harvest enough apples to last most of the winter.

Twice a week I'd venture down to Laytonville to retrieve the contents of PO Box 1000, the number that had been serendipitously assigned to me when the new post office opened. Somebody or something must have been telling me I was destined to go into the mail order business.

I was receiving so many orders for records and magazines that the box was usually stuffed beyond capacity. I worried about getting on the wrong side of the post office staff, and wondered what they must think about the often bizarrely illustrated letters and fanzines that arrived for me.

But apart from a quizzical but friendly raised eyebrow now and then, the clerks remained utterly unfazed. When there was too much mail to fit into my box, they'd decant it into foot-deep plastic trays and hand them across the counter with a cheery, "Got your work cut out for you this week!" or "Looks like business is booming!"

It was. Mail order accounted for only 10% of Lookout Records' total sales, but it was by far the most labor-intensive aspect of running the label. I'd never done this kind of work before, but there was enough variety to the letters and orders to keep it from getting boring. I worked out systems, figured out how to create a computerized mailing list, and bragged in our ads and press releases that the entire operation was solar-powered.

Regrettably, I was no longer able to say the same thing about our band. Tre and Kain's families had both moved to Willits, so we now did most of our practicing in a studio Tre's dad built for us at the back of their new house. It was convenient to have limitless amounts of city electricity at our disposal, but it would never be the same as on the mountain, where we could play as loudly and as long into the night as we wanted.

Of course there'd been a time the previous winter when we almost died doing just that. Several hours of jamming on a dirge-like hymn about environmental apocalypse had drained the solar-powered batteries, forcing me to turn on the generator. Engrossed as we were with the song's repetitive rhythms and subtle permutations, it didn't seem that remarkable when an eerie orange light began dancing on the walls in time to the music.

But when the light grew bright enough to cast shadows, shadows that then threw themselves into the dance, I began to wonder if this phenomenon might be the result of something other than a magical presence we had conjured up. Turning to look out the window, I saw that the shed was engulfed in flames.

The generator had come loose from its mounting and rolled up against the shed door, where the heat from its exhaust pipe set the wood alight. That was bad enough; what made it much, much worse was that I had a couple dozen gallons of gas stored only a few feet away. If the flames reached the gas cans, the resulting fireball would easily envelop the house.

Tearing out the door, grabbing the hose as I went, I struggled frantically to extinguish the fire before it was too late. If it had been cold enough that night for the water in the hose to be frozen, or if a couple more minutes had elapsed before I spotted the flames, we might not be here today. At the very least, the house wouldn't.

But for the most part it was a crisis-free time on the mountain, a time that came closest to living up to the fantasies of rural life that had led me there in the first place. On summer evenings, I'd take my radio up into the marijuana patch, where I'd sit examining the flowers, plucking away at dead leaves, and basking in the rich skunky perfume that hung lazily over the hillside.

Now that KMUD had built a new signal tower, it came in loud and clear, and I listened to the station almost nonstop. One of my favorite programs, hosted by two Irish women, was *Hot Potatoes*. It featured Celtic music that had mostly originated in the Emerald Isle but felt equally at home in the Emerald Triangle. The sound of its lilting fiddles and loping drumbeats echoing down the canyon remains among the fondest of all my Spy Rock memories.

If I had to travel to the Bay Area to meet with bands or do

recording work, I'd park my truck under a tree in some obscure corner of San Francisco and sleep in the camper shell. But most of my business could be handled closer to home. My "office" became a phone booth in the parking lot of Grapewine Station (formerly Czech Lodge, scene of the first Lookouts show), just off Highway 101.

Friends at the Shred of Dignity skate collective in San Francisco had let me install a phone line and answering machine in their warehouse. Armed with a bag of quarters, I'd drive the 10 miles down to Grapewine Station, call the answering machine to retrieve my messages, and spend the rest of the afternoon returning calls.

This system had drawbacks, like the passing semi trucks that frequently drowned out conversations. Equally problematic were those individuals—especially in Los Angeles—who couldn't get their heads around the idea that there was a place where people weren't immediately reachable—or reachable at all—by phone.

"Can I speak to _____?" I'd say.

"Give me your number and I'll have him call you back."

"That won't work, there aren't any phones where I live. I need to talk to him now, before I drive back up the mountain."

It wasn't unusual to get hung up on at that point. Eventually receptionists at the pressing plant and mastering lab got used to my strange ways and put me straight through, but there was always potential for crossed wires and misunderstandings when contacting people unfamiliar with how I operated.

During one of those afternoon sessions, I got a message from John Kiffmeyer, aka Al Sobrante (a tribute to his home town of El Sobrante). Al had been the drummer and a chief driving force behind Isocracy, one of the first Lookout bands. He wanted to tell me about the new band he'd joined with two teenagers from the far-flung East Bay suburb of Rodeo.

"They don't know that much about punk," he said, "but they're really good. Got any shows we can play?"

There was one coming up, but it didn't sound that promising. Without bothering to consult Kain or me, Tre had committed the Lookouts to playing some high school party at a cabin in the hills above Willits.

We'd played for high school kids before. It was usually a hit or miss situation. As often as not, the kids would show no interest in our music, being preoccupied with drinking, flirting, and whatever else teenagers do at parties. Once in a while, though, we'd get an audience that genuinely appreciated us.

Still, a show was a show. I told Al about it. "There's no money, it's in the middle of nowhere, it'll take you three or four hours to get there, and if it snows like it's supposed to, the whole thing might get called off."

"We'll be there," he said.

The weather turned out almost as bad as I'd feared. There wasn't much snow, but swatches of ice left the upper reaches of Sherwood Road unusually treacherous. It's said in Mendocino County that you don't go driving up Spy Rock Road unless you know where you're going and have legitimate business there. Sherwood Road, especially the remote stretch where we were headed, is kind of the same deal.

On arriving, we found three kids shivering outside a locked cabin. The kid whose party it was—and who had the keys—had decided to stay in town because it was "too cold." Two more kids showed up, swelling our potential audience to five, but that was it. It seemed like a shame to have come all this distance and not play, but what were we supposed to do if we couldn't even get inside?

Just then a van drove up, and I heard Al Sobrante's

unmistakable voice boom out, "What's going on? Let's get this show on the road!"

Al's new band was called Sweet Children. The two younger guys, both 16 (Al was three years older) almost did seem like children: quiet, kind of bashful, content to let Al do most of the talking. The tall, lanky bass player was named Mike; the guitarist, whose long, curly hair partially concealed his face, introduced himself as Billie Joe.

I won't say whose idea this was—partly because I'm not sure the statute of limitations has expired, mostly because I honestly don't remember—but *somebody* suggested we break into the cabin and start a fire in the stove before we all froze to death. And *somebody*—again, I'm not sure who—did just that.

Once inside and thawed out, it seemed like we might as well go ahead with the show. The cabin had no lights, but there were plenty of candles, and we found a generator out back to power the bands. Sweet Children took the "stage"—some cleared-out floor space near the front door—and played for the five high school kids sitting politely at their feet.

I watched from the back, only half paying attention at first. But before they'd finished even one song, I was absolutely riveted. I'd seen this level of performance before, but only in giant, packed arenas or stadiums, delivered by bands at the peak of their careers. Sixteen-year-old Billie Joe exuded the casual self-confidence of a superstar, offset slightly but not entirely by a shy, self-effacing humility.

Stopping every few songs to thank his minuscule audience, he sang and played as though he'd been doing this all his life— which, I would learn, wasn't far from the truth. Walking up to me afterward, he offhandedly asked, "What did you think?"

"I want to make a record with you guys," was all I could say.

They were barely getting started—this might have been

their third or fourth show ever—but I'd seen and heard all I needed to. They were like a modern, updated, punk rock version of the Beatles. They could seriously be that big, I caught myself thinking. Crazy talk? Of course. Yet at that moment it made perfect, undeniable sense.

The Lookouts never played that night; by the time Sweet Children finished, it was midnight and our "audience," worried they'd get in trouble with their parents, said goodbye and headed home. On the long drive back to Spy Rock, twisting the radio dial in search of an audible signal and thankful for my aging truck's slightly more than adequate heater, I had barely an inkling of how the night's events were about to change my life forever.

nine

nine

And everything did change, not all at once, not in obvious, visible ways at first, but the wheels were in motion. Life on Spy Rock unfolded peacefully and quietly through the rest of 1988 and into 1989. I barely noticed winter that year; spring was bright and full of promise.

The Sweet Children record was nearly done. They'd gone into the studio at the end of the year, and by March we had everything in place for a four-song EP. Just as I was about to print the covers and labels, they casually informed me that they'd decided to change their name to Green Day.

I blew a gasket. It was too late, I told them; there was no time to redo all the artwork. On top of that, I demanded, how was I supposed to sell a record by a band no one had heard of? "Green Day?" I sneered. "What's it even supposed to mean?"

But as is often the case with bands, they'd decided what they wanted and that was going to be that. Thanks to my 24-hour copy shop connection, we managed to pull an all-nighter, throw together a new cover, and the record came out on time. It didn't sell much at first, but I'd expected that. Sweet Children/Green Day were a slight departure from the usual Lookout Records fare: poppier, more melodic, almost, dare I say, a little mainstream.

I loved the record, but it was far from the only thing on my mind. Operation Ivy, Lookout's biggest band, had been struggling to produce their first album for over a year. They'd come close to finishing it once, only to decide they didn't like how it sounded and to start all over with a new producer. Finally, though, it looked like it was going to happen—if, that is, we could coax the cover art out of Jesse, their gifted but mercurial singer.

Meanwhile, the Lookouts were putting the final touches on a new album, too. Considering the problems I'd had four years earlier, with crazed hippies threatening to burn down my house for bringing too much attention to the area, the title I chose could have made it seem like I was just begging for trouble. But times had changed, and I never thought of calling it anything other than *Spy Rock Road.*

The cover art both lampooned and paid tribute to our mountain home, with a panoramic portrayal of rampaging lumberjacks, CAMP helicopter cowboys, marching stormtroopers, a punk rock band with their amps plugged into a pine tree, and a stray bullet whizzing through the Spy Rock Road sign. It was the work of the mysterious "M," who, tucked away in an anonymous corner of the county, had long been contributing incendiary editorial cartoons to Boonville's *Anderson Valley Advertiser*, and, more recently, to the *Lookout* as well.

If any of my neighbors had complaints about the cover, they kept them to themselves. A few even offered compliments. *Lookout* magazine had firmly established itself as part of the cultural landscape; now even the Lookouts were becoming semi-respectable.

I might not have realized it at the time, but my work at KMUD was doing wonders in helping me graduate from former pariah to full-fledged member of the community. I was putting almost as much time and energy into my commitments there as I was into the magazine and record label: sitting in for other DJs, hosting public affairs programs, attending staff meetings, and becoming an avid fundraiser.

Not content with hectoring listeners for donations during our semiannual pledge drives, I began looking into other ways to raise money for the station. Since our Lookout Records-based show had done so well in Arcata, I decided to put on another one in Garberville, this time as a KMUD benefit.

Garberville was not, to put it mildly, a hot spot on the punk rock touring circuit. The Los Angeles-based band X had come through in 1983, and there'd been a dry spell after that of about six years, broken only when Chris Appelgren and I organized a couple of shows at the beginning of 1989.

One of them, a February show featuring the Lookouts and my Pope-terrorizing San Francisco flatmates, MDC, had been a huge success, apart from Tre dislocating his knee while trying to impress girls by doing power slides in the snow and having to spend the night in the hospital.

Convinced that the bill I had planned—Operation Ivy, Screeching Weasel, Green Day, and the Lookouts—would draw an even bigger crowd, I assured a skeptical KMUD management that I'd take care of everything, that they need only stand by and wait for the money to roll in.

Two unfortunate things happened on the way to this big payday. First, Operation Ivy broke up. I begged them to put aside their differences long enough to play this show, but they'd already decided to say their goodbyes at Gilman Street a couple weeks earlier.

Second, just when I was daring to believe that the blue-eyed rastas and terminal Deadheads might be losing their grip on the Southern Humboldt music scene, the granddaddy of all Deadheads, Jerry Garcia himself, threw me a curve by booking a show a few miles down the road on the same night as mine.

A couple years later, either Screeching Weasel or Green Day could have filled any Vets Hall in the land, Jerry Garcia or no

Jerry Garcia, but on June 10, 1989, in Garberville, California, this was not the case. Even adding the Mr. T Experience, who had a decent following in the Bay Area but were largely unknown up our way, didn't help.

People often ask how somebody like Jerry Garcia, playing a completely different style of music, could steal away our punk rock audience. But that's how Southern Humboldt was: in such a small community, with relatively few opportunities to see live music, people couldn't afford to cordon themselves off into cliques, genres, and subcultures as rigidly as they did in big cities.

So it wasn't considered at all strange for kids to attend a Jerry Garcia show one night and a punk rock show the next. Unfortunately, if the two happened on the same night, Jerry was always going to win. In the end, the Vets Hall wasn't much more than half filled, and not only did KMUD not make any money, I wound up losing a good chunk of my own.

It was still a memorable show, even if having to spend the night worrying about cash and logistics took some of the fun out of it for me. Mike Dirnt, Green Day's bassist, had been drinking heavily (I got the impression that, at 17, it wasn't something he was used to). When it came time for him to play, he was outside puking in the bushes.

We half-led, half-carried him to the stage, and helped him find his bass (he hadn't noticed it was strapped across his shoulders). Thinking he'd be lucky to manage more than a couple of songs, I was ready to cut Green Day's set short, but from the instant the first chord was struck, Mike was a man transformed. He may not have been able to see beyond the end of his nose, might not even have been too sure where he was, but he played from a place where mistakes were unheard of and wrong notes nonexistent.

Screeching Weasel, completely sober, didn't fare so well. Ben Weasel, their acerbic frontman, worked his usual schtick of trying to coax a reaction out of the audience with a series of taunts and insults, but the hippie-tinged punks of Garberville weren't buying it. Or even getting it, for that matter.

Ben's material consisted largely of in-jokes that would make sense only to *MRR*-reading devotees of "the scene." The sunny-faced Humboldt kids stared blankly back at his acid-tongued Led Zeppelin-baiting as if to ask, "Dude, why is that guy having such a *bummer*?"

Ben's bummer did not diminish when he and the band had to follow me up Spy Rock to spend the night. They were city people, driving a city car. Mile after mile of precipitous unpaved roads, devoid of streetlights or Burger Kings, did not compute. His next *MRR* column began, "What kind of asshole lives nine miles up the side of a goddam mountain?"

Green Day made the trip up Spy Rock, too, without complaints or comments, except for the next morning when Billie and Mike griped that my "ferocious" dogs had kept them trapped in their van all night. "Ruf-Ruf and Kong?" I marveled. "I guess maybe they could have licked you to death."

Driving back down to Berkeley, I insisted we make a quick stop in Laytonville. I wanted the bands to see something of my world, a world they'd so often heard me talk about. I had another, not quite so honorable motive: I knew it would drive Ben Weasel right up the wall.

It was the weekend of the annual Laytonville Rodeo, and our normally quiet little crossroads was abuzz with life, the kind of life I was certain Ben would not have encountered back in Chicago. We found ourselves sandwiched between half a dozen cowboys on horseback and a flatbed truck carrying a similar number of hill muffins in dazzling day-glo and tie-dye.

The icing on the cake was provided by a gaggle of jugglers and clowns from Camp Winnarainbow.

Camp Winnarainbow was a performing arts camp for children and young-at-heart adults, situated on land north of Laytonville owned by the Hog Farm, a long-running hippie commune. Its founder, Hugh "Wavy Gravy" Romney, is probably best known as the disembodied voice warning Woodstock attendees to avoid the brown acid.

People had been dubious when the camp was launched—who was going to pay to have their kids looked after by a bunch of legendary stoners?—but Camp Winnarainbow had grown into one of Laytonville's most profitable non-drug-related-businesses.

My niece and nephew, like many local children, spent time there. So, to the everlasting shame of the Lookouts, did our drummer. In fact, Tre was still summering at Camp Winnarainbow well into his teens. If we had a show, we'd have to drive in and retrieve him from whatever drum circle or mime class he was engaged in. "Aren't you a little old for this?" I'd complain, to which he'd retort, "Never too old for having fun!"

Ben Weasel, as I'd anticipated, did not enjoy the sights and sounds of the Laytonville Rodeo. He had fixed and often highly arbitrary ideas about how the world should be ordered. Within this scheme of things, there was little room for clowns, hippies, and cowboys, especially not all jumbled together in one place. He sat there silently fuming, convinced, no doubt, that I, in cahoots with the whole town of Laytonville, had cooked up this concoction of clashing cultures for the sole purpose of tormenting him.

Punk rock remained at the center of my personal and professional life, but my explorations of the North Coast's backwoods and byways and my growing affection for homegrown culture were bringing me into contact with music and musicians I previously would have ignored or avoided.

There was Indiana Slim, of course, who, despite the inadvertent role he'd played in the Piano Jimmy punchout, had gone out of his way to befriend me at a time when I'd most needed it. I'd never cared much for blues or blues-based rock, especially when played by white guys, but Slim imbued his work—and his life—with such infectious enthusiasm that it was hard not to be a fan.

He and his wife, Baby Lee, cruised around in a wildly impractical gold Cadillac, complete with the giant tailfins of an earlier, more profligate era. Slim was a walking, talking monument to the age of hepcats and crazy jive, while Baby Lee radiated a star quality that would have been at home anywhere from a two-bit honky-tonk to Carnegie Hall. Which made it all the more discombobulating to encounter them in the Laytonville Post Office parking lot.

I never figured out—nor did I have the nerve to ask—exactly where and how they lived. I had a hard time picturing Slim swapping his ebony winklepickers and gold lamé sport coat for rubber boots and a rain suit to dig out a blocked culvert. I preferred to believe mundane rural realities never intruded into what looked like their charmed movie star existence.

Through Slim I met Michael Ferretta, a singer-songwriter with an acoustic guitar and an in-your-face attitude that could have been called folk-punk if the term had existed at the time. He was something of a mountain troubadour, especially beloved by the growers and their families. "Locked Gates And A Loaded .45," lamenting the paranoia and violence that had invaded the once-peaceful pot trade, was his signature tune and an instantly recognizable local anthem.

He, his wife, their three children, and Michael's elderly father occupied an expanded, modernized version of the log cabin his grandfather had built early in the 20th century. They were homeschooling their kids, who seemed years ahead of their contemporaries, both academically and socially.

I'd met other homeschoolers, including the Colfaxes of Anderson Valley, who'd gained national attention when three of their sons were admitted to Harvard without ever having set foot in a conventional classroom, but the Ferrettas were the first I was able to observe up close.

They were dead serious about education, establishing study hours and assignments more rigorous than anything the kids would have encountered in the Laytonville public schools. As the kids grew older, the adult Ferrettas often had to revisit their own studies to keep up.

Homeschooling was much discussed and debated among mountain families. A perennial question was whether stay-at-home kids missed out on the "socialization" process that a conventional school offers. To its proponents, socialization meant learning to work, play, and interact with one's peers, but depending on one's own experience at school—mine, for example, had not been a good one—it could also be seen as bullying, ostracizing, and singling out for attack anyone who deviated from the norm.

But not every parent claiming to be a homeschooler was motivated by sound principles and values. Some kept their kids at home to save themselves the trouble and expense of shuttling them down the mountain to catch the school bus. Others were indifferent or actively hostile to the concept of education itself, seeing it as a brainwashing tool of "the man."

"Kids are smart, they can learn on their own," they'd insist, then proceed to smoke, snort, or drink themselves into oblivion while their children effectively ran wild. On our mountain alone there were at least half a dozen functionally and socially illiterate young people who grew up without acquiring the skills they'd need should they want to leave the mountain and try their hand at modern life.

The discovery that children could be as badly miseducated outside the school system as in it chipped away at my long-standing anti-authoritarian attitudes. I began giving serious thought and study to how education should work. This led to the first of several "theme" issues of the *Lookout*. The cover was as irreverent and iconoclastic as ever—a headline shouting, "HEY STUPID! WERE YOU BORN LIKE THAT OR DID YOU LEARN IT IN SCHOOL?"—but inside was some of the most serious journalism I'd ever attempted.

I interviewed Bruce Anderson, editor and publisher of Boonville's much renowned and reviled *Anderson Valley Advertiser*. Anderson, a burly, outspoken man with a coruscating, Menckenesque sense of humor, hadn't limited his critique of the educational establishment to routinely lambasting it in print. He'd made his point still more emphatically by punching out the Mendocino County Superintendent of Schools, which had earned him 90 days in the county slammer.

For a countervailing opinion, I brought in Laytonville school chief Brian Buckley, who bent over backward to be conciliatory and reasonable, two qualities of the local liberal ruling class that, when wielded in defense of the status quo, most infuriated a fire-breathing radical like Bruce.

I devoted a couple of pages to an anonymous homeschooling family—I guess after all this time it's okay to reveal it was the Ferrettas—and rounded off the issue with my politically progressive, socially conservative uncle who'd spent his life as an educator, and whose idealism and enthusiasm, even at 80, remained remarkably undimmed.

I was surprised—a little astounded, even—at how well the new issue was received. People who'd once refused even to look at the *Lookout* were quoting things I'd said, and other publications (besides the *AVA*, which had been doing it for years) began reprinting my articles. Organizations and institutions sent me press releases and announcements as if I were a bona fide member of the media establishment, which, at least by Mendocino County standards, I suppose I was.

Records, books, and magazines came flooding in, too, and no longer just from punk rockers. Most of them went into my "I'll get around to it one of these days" pile, but a cassette called *I Had To Be Born This Century* by one Darryl Cherney caught both my eye and my ear.

Cherney, despite his folksy, good-old-boy drawl and country-tinged musical style, was new on the scene, recently arrived from New York City's Upper West Side. You never would have guessed it from listening to him, though, nor even when meeting him, which I did, shortly after giving his tape an enthusiastic review in the *Lookout*.

I found him and his partner, Judi Bari, living in a cabin that was, just as he'd described it in his song about the great Eel River flood of 1986, "a hundred yards from the water's edge." Judi was a musician, too, and she and Darryl often performed together, but her real talent was political organizing. She and Darryl were driving forces behind the North Coast chapter of Earth First!

Most people thought of one thing and one thing only when they heard the name Earth First!: tree-spiking. In reality, the loose-knit group—so loose-knit that it was sometimes more of a concept than an actual organization—advocated a wide range of tactics.

Some of those tactics did include "ecotage" or "monkey-wrenching"—pouring sand into a bulldozer's crankcase, for example—while others emphasized traditional civil disobedience techniques like picket lines and sit-ins. But nothing struck fear into the hearts of forest workers—or evoked their anger—like the threat of spikes or nails being driven into trees to make them unharvestable.

Earth First! would eventually disavow tree-spiking, but it hadn't yet done so in 1987, when a Sonoma County millworker was nearly decapitated after his saw blade hit a nail in the log he was working on. That incident ratcheted up tensions between environmentalists and loggers to the point where violence felt like a near-constant possibility.

Looking back now, I regret not making more of an effort to understand the loggers' point of view. Until the arrival of marijuana, their industry had completely dominated the North Coast. It paid well, and in light of the densely forested mountains that surrounded us in every direction, it's easy to see why people assumed there was a never-ending supply of logs to be cut and milled.

They hadn't counted on a couple of factors. One was modern technology, which allowed forests to be cut far faster than had ever been possible before, and another was globalization, which created a market where raw logs by the tens of thousands could be shipped overseas to developing markets instead of being milled at home.

When, as a result, local sawmills began closing down and laying off employees, the corporations who owned most of the timberland used the resulting fear and insecurity to whip up hostility toward "environmental extremists" who, they claimed, were trying to eliminate logging altogether.

In reality, the corporations, spurred by the need to pay off massive debts accrued in the course of hostile takeovers, had set about liquidating their assets (i.e., the forests) as quickly as possible. It was true that logging was in danger of becoming extinct on the North Coast; the bitter irony was that the logging companies themselves were driving the final nails into its coffin.

Like many newcomers to the land, especially those who had never had to depend on the forest products industry for a living, I was almost viscerally opposed to logging. I became even more so when I did research into the long-term and, in some cases, irreversible damage caused by widespread clearcutting. I won't claim my views were sophisticated or nuanced, but they were definitely impassioned.

So when a coalition of environmentalists announced a summer of protest and civil disobedience aimed at slowing down or stopping the wholesale logging of the last of the North Coast's old growth redwoods, I jumped right on board. Originally billed as "Mississippi Summer in the California Redwoods," the concept was based on 1964's "Freedom Summer," when activists from around the country descended on Mississippi to challenge its Jim Crow laws and register African-Americans to vote.

As much as I liked the idea, I questioned its image and approach. The "Mississippi Summer" name felt awkward and unwieldy, and would be next to meaningless for young activists who might not even have been born in 1964. I argued in favor of calling it "Redwood Summer," on grounds that it was catchier, more succinct, and to the point.

Darryl and Judi, who'd taken a lead role in planning the protests, agreed, but thought it would be more trouble than it was worth to persuade other coalition members, many of whom framed every political action in the rhetoric and style of their beloved 1960s, that a name change was in order. I took matters into my own hands, using every opportunity, in print or on the radio, to refer to it as "Redwood Summer." It still felt like a losing battle until I collaborated with the *AVA*'s "M" to create a poster for the event.

While I can barely draw a rudimentary stick figure, I can sometimes come up with concepts that an actual artist—and "M" was an especially gifted one—can turn into reality. I don't remember how much of the picture—a protester with an outstretched hand stopping a logging truck—was my idea, but I furnished the tag line, "It's been said the 90s will make the 60s look like the 50s," followed by, in larger print: "THIS IS WHERE THE 90s BEGIN."

But my crucial contribution was convincing "M" to replace "Mississippi Summer In The California Redwoods" with "Redwood Summer." By the time the poster had been reproduced and circulated across the country, the "Mississippi" coinage was dead and gone.

I distributed several thousand copies by way of *Lookout* magazine, Lookout Records mail orders, Bay Area punk shows, bookshops, food co-ops, and anywhere else my travels took me. I don't know how much my efforts had to do with it, but Redwood Summer wound up attracting a small but noticeable contingent of punks, who once wouldn't have been caught dead anywhere near such a brazenly "hippie" event.

Prominent among them was former Dead Kennedys frontman Jello Biafra, who'd been brought to Mendocino County by artist Winston Smith, a longtime friend and collaborator. Winston, despite being widely known in the punk world for his album covers and stridently seditious collage works, had lived for many years on a communal ranch near Ukiah.

Biafra might have originally come to speak on behalf of

the trees, but he was soon devoting at least as much energy to touting the medicinal and economic benefits of "hemp."

It had become an article of faith among the hippies, especially in the wilder-eyed precincts of the Emerald Triangle, that the true value of marijuana extended far beyond its traditional purposes of getting high and making a living. It was also a medicine, we were told, one capable of alleviating or curing everything from backache and depression to cancer and AIDS.

What's more, hemp oil would soon replace fossil fuels as our chief energy source, and hemp fibers would provide us with more environmentally efficient paper, clothing, and building materials. The only reason it remained illegal, the story went, was because of pressure exerted on the government by corporations desperate to protect their profits. I signed on to this theory as wholeheartedly as Biafra had, feeling no need to look too deeply into the "evidence" behind it.

Despite crusading on behalf of the marijuana industry, I was becoming less and less fond of actually smoking the stuff. I hadn't given it up altogether, though it often occurred to me that I should. But after more than two decades—I'd smoked my first joint in 1967—of believing that it heightened my consciousness and made me a more spiritual and moral being, I was starting to suspect the drug was doing me no favors.

Having seen too much of my time and energy vanish into a dope-inflected haze, I tried to curtail my usage. I'd be successful for a while; then, like a classic amnesiac, would forget my best intentions and rationalize that adding a little "edge" or "buzz" to the morning would make everything more enjoyable and productive.

Ten minutes later, often before the sun had cleared the trees and with the clock still lumbering its way toward 7 or 8 am, I'd be cursing my stupidity and accepting that another day had disappeared down the drain. At times like this I'd wonder if the solitude was finally getting to me.

What with the record label, the band, the magazine, the radio station, and my new political work, I was meeting and interacting with more people than I ever had in my life, but I always came back to my mountain redoubt alone, resigned to the likelihood of living a hermit's life forever.

There might have been legitimate reasons for my discouragement, but looking back now, it's easy to see how marijuana was making things worse. It left me feeling lazy and stupid, and encouraged me to hang out in my own private universe, a fine place to be when you hanker to reign supreme and run roughshod over reality, but a lonely, futile place if you're hoping to hook up with another human being.

During the years I'd been growing marijuana, I'd been able to smoke as much of it as I wanted, but my days as a grower would soon be at an end. The record label was too big now, too much of a legitimate business for me to be doing anything shady on the side. If, God forbid, I ever got raided, the authorities would almost surely assume the label's finances were being underwritten by drug money.

In reality they were not; the label had been self-sustaining since the beginning. But convincing the cops or the taxman of that would be a tough sell. I—and the bands I'd been entrusted to, pardon the expression, look out for—could lose everything.

Up till then I'd solved the problem of keeping my illicit business and my legit one separate by having my partner David handle Lookout's finances and paperwork. But he'd announced he was quitting at the end of the year. It had become "too much like a job," he told me. The upshot was that if I wanted to keep the label in business (at this point I wasn't totally sure if I did),

I was going to have to emerge from the underground and start treading the straight and narrow.

These were the sorts of things running through my mind as the achingly beautiful autumn of 1989 slipped softly away. On one hand, I'd never been happier with Spy Rock and its way of life; on the other, I felt a nagging suspicion that something was not quite right, that everything might soon be coming undone.

On an exquisitely sunny and warm October day I was cutting firewood and listening to the World Series game between the San Francisco Giants and the Oakland A's when the radio suddenly broke into a play-by-play of the Loma Prieta earthquake. As was usually the case when natural disasters struck "down below," I felt like I was floating safely above it all.

At times like that I could barely imagine wanting to leave this wonderful, almost perfect world. But even in my moments of greatest contentment, I sensed a time might be coming when I would have no choice.

Angst and unsettledness continued to be interspersed with moments of magic. Rolling down the mountain shortly after sunrise, I popped the new Lookouts album into the tape deck and my favorite song came blasting forth:

And the rain still falls on the green hills of England
And the sun beats down on our California home
And the wind blows free across all your borders
Why must we be always on the run?

I'd written it a couple years earlier while stranded on the side of an English country lane by a downpour of such astonishing ferocity that it made driving impossible. The rain blotted out the landscape to the point where I imagined I could see the shapes of ancient Roman warriors driving native Celts and Britons west into the wilds of Cornwall and Wales.

Was it too great a stretch, I wondered, to liken that civilizational clash to our own government's "war" against modern-day tribes of hippies and back-to-the-landers on one of the last frontiers of the American Empire? Not that it mattered; this was a polemical punk rock song I was writing, not the sequel to Gibbon's *Decline And Fall*.

In any event, that chorus summed up much of what my life had been about these past several years. In every direction, as far as I could see, the green hills of Mendocino were transfixed upon my eyes and transfigured in my soul. This was my home, my heart, my destiny. I could no more leave it than it could leave me. It was a moment, I felt, destined to become a touchstone for all that mattered, for the rest of my life.

The year glided to a gentle conclusion. On New Year's Eve, the Lookouts spent the afternoon at KMUD, clowning around and playing soft, acoustic versions of our normally abrasive songs. They felt well suited to the day, mild and swathed in a not unpleasant cloud of melancholy and nostalgia.

Midway through "That Girl's From Outer Space," Kain's upright bass "exploded," as I described it over the air, though what actually happened was that the bridge snapped loose, sending strings flying every which way.

Instead of cursing our luck or feeling our performance was ruined, we laughed hysterically while the bass was reassembled, then played some more, until we'd all but run out of songs. Chris, who'd been manning the control board, faded into an extended version of "Disco Inferno," and we spilled out onto the parking lot to say our goodbyes.

It was only then that I remembered it wasn't just any New Year we were celebrating, but the turn of a decade. At the beginning of the 1980s, I'd been fearful, almost despondent, about the direction I saw my life going; ten years down the line, I was brimming over with optimism and excitement.

1990. It really felt like the future now. Like science fiction, almost. Who would have dreamed I'd live this long and still have so much to live for? I knew before it began that 1990 was going to be a banner year, something that would prove to be true in almost every way. What I didn't know, what I couldn't or wouldn't have wanted to know, was that it would also mark the beginning of the end of my time on Spy Rock Road.

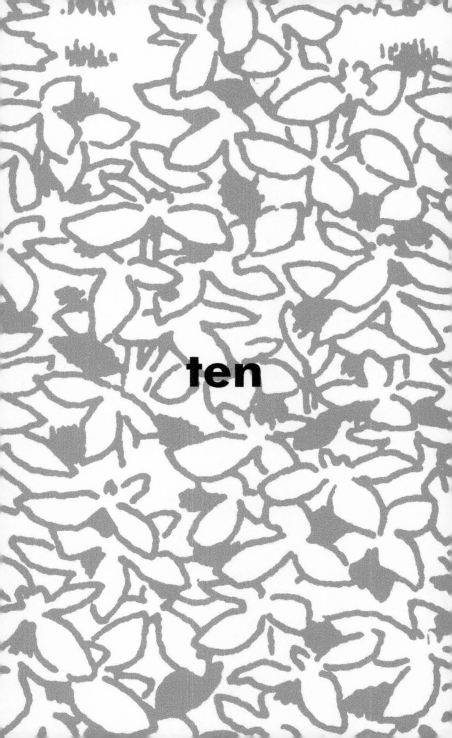

ten

CAMP's best efforts to wipe out the marijuana trade had succeeded only in driving prices higher, to double or triple what they had once been. Farmers who'd been smart or lucky enough to survive the raids were reaping undreamed of bonanzas. Laytonville was even turning into a bit of a boomtown.

It was no longer just the growers getting rich. Businesses that provided them with the tools of their trade and the luxury goods they could now afford were prospering as well. Skyrocketing prices prompted even the most upright citizens, who'd never dreamed of consorting with hippies, to throw a few plants in the ground themselves.

But although I had finally begun to get halfway good at growing marijuana, I had no regrets about getting out of the business. It proved to be the right decision. I no longer had the time, energy, or inclination to look after my plants. Nor did I need the paranoia and pressure that came with even a small-time operation.

This was especially true now that I was running Lookout Records entirely from Spy Rock. As he'd said he would, David Hayes had left at the beginning of the year. Still uncertain whether I'd be able to manage on my own, I'd hired my 17-year-old KMUD co-host Chris Appelgren to help out on weekends.

Chris would eventually develop into a top-class artist and illustrator, but at the time was still in the early learning-to-draw stages of his career. That, along with menial chores like stuffing 7" records into sleeves, took up all the hours he could spare.

Everything else was up to me. Within months my initial fears had dissipated. Having once believed that David's knowledge and experience were indispensable, I found that things actually operated more smoothly without the constant bickering that had crept into our relationship during the last two years we worked together.

In April, Chris and I traveled down to Gilman Street to celebrate the simultaneous release of records by Green Day, Neurosis, the Mr. T Experience, and Samiam. Any one of these would have been an event in itself, so we were expecting a decently attended show, but were astounded to find lines stretching around the block long before the doors opened.

It was the first time I genuinely felt—in more than a wishful way—that Lookout was becoming a "big" deal. Chris and I had little time to enjoy the music; we spent the night behind the merchandise table with people thrusting fistfuls of money at us until they'd bought every record and t-shirt we had to sell.

As we drove back to Spy Rock not long before dawn, we were still pulling wads of bills out of every available pocket. If the cops had happened to stop us—as practically the only vehicle on the highway we made an obvious target—they could hardly have been blamed for thinking we'd just pulled off some massively successful drug deal.

The money coming in from Lookout wasn't enough to provide me with a fulltime living, but it no longer seemed far-fetched to imagine that one day it might. No matter how much things might be looking up, though, I spent too much time worrying about the future. Not just in a material sense— though that was always on my mind—but existentially as well.

In my 40s now, I was plagued by fears that I might spend the rest of my life in a never-ending scramble to make ends meet. Beneath those nagging worries lay a deeper discontent:

the notion that time was running out on me, that if I were ever going to do something important or worthwhile with my life, I'd better get started on it. Even if I had no idea what "it" might be.

When I tried to explain this to others, I was met with blank stares or outright derision. Most people thought what I was doing was important and worthwhile enough. Lookout, they said, was providing an invaluable service, doing it honestly and fairly, and enabling dozens of young musicians and artists to reach an ever more receptive public.

Letters that I got from kids in far-flung places echoed this sentiment. Many cited Lookout as a life-changing inspiration. Yet as much as I loved the music, and the people and energy it was bringing me into contact with, I had trouble taking it seriously. The guilt-ridden and martyrdom-seeking version of Catholicism I'd grown up with might have had something to do with it. Nothing, my conscience hinted, could be this much fun without being morally suspect.

It was time, I kept thinking, that I got a "real" job, the kind of job my parents could tell neighbors and relatives about without having to fudge the truth or apologize. Racking my brains for something, anything I might be qualified for, I remembered that earlier in life, before bombing out of multiple colleges, I'd wanted to be a teacher.

The time and effort required to obtain a teaching credential, not to mention my inability to show up on a regular basis for anything resembling work, had long since put that dream out of reach. Or so I thought, until someone pointed out that it was much easier to qualify as a substitute teacher. Better yet, substitutes only worked when and if they chose to.

Apart from passing a basic competency exam—I'd always been good at tests—all I needed was a bachelor's degree. When my most recent attempt at higher education had crashed and burned in the mid-70s, I'd been a year—two at most—short of graduating.

It looked like the perfect solution. I could work two or three days a week doing something both I and society at large could agree was "respectable." I'd have the rest of my time free for the record label and the magazine. Financial and self-esteem problems solved in one fell swoop!

I was sure I'd be an excellent teacher, since there were few things I enjoyed more than hearing myself talk. I didn't stop to wonder whether my students would feel the same way. My overconfidence was further inflated when a Eureka High School teacher marveled at how many teenage readers the *Lookout* seemed to attract.

"I can't get them to open a book, but all over the school I see them with their noses buried in that magazine of yours. What's your secret?" he asked.

"Write about interesting things," I said breezily, discounting intrinsic kid-magnets like the irreverence, profanity, and simplistic sloganeering that often characterized the *Lookout*. It never occurred to me that young people might not be similarly entranced if I were trying to explain ancient history or English grammar.

Just like that, it was decided. I was going to be a teacher. Part-time, and only when I felt like it, but a teacher nevertheless. The downside was that I'd have to leave the mountain to go back to college. Once I was finished, though, the money I'd be earning, along with my record label income, would ensure that I'd never have to leave again.

I'd failed in every previous attempt at college, but couldn't see why it would be a problem this time. Decades of pumping up my self-esteem by various means, many of them chemical, had convinced me I already knew most things worth knowing.

A college degree, in my estimation, would be mostly a matter of jumping through the right hoops and filling out a bit of paperwork.

Viewed in that light, it seemed logical to choose the college that would be fastest, easiest, and cheapest to breeze through. Humboldt State, up in Arcata, fit the bill. It enjoyed a semi-decent academic reputation, I knew people there, I liked the town, and, best of all, I wouldn't have to leave the North Coast.

But despite being technically "in the area," Arcata was two and a half hours away, so daily commuting wouldn't be a realistic option. I'd be able to get home for weekends and the occasional daytrip, but I'd still have to find a place to live near campus.

My other option was Berkeley. It was where I'd last studied, and though the work had been hard—and a constant challenge to my belief that I already knew most of what was worth knowing—I'd enjoyed my time there.

If I hadn't gotten involved in some body-and-soul-destroying drug abuse, I would have graduated with a degree in Asian Studies and moderate fluency in Chinese, well positioned for any number of careers in the USA or abroad. Instead, I was sitting on a mountain in the middle of nowhere, selling punk rock records and wondering what to do with my life.

Berkeley would be my only choice if I wanted to resume my Asian Studies program, but in the 14 years since I'd last darkened the door of a college classroom, I'd forgotten most of my Chinese and a big chunk of everything else. I'd basically be starting over, almost from scratch.

No longer harboring dreams of a new life in the Far East, all I wanted now was a piece of paper declaring me a college graduate. For that purpose, Humboldt State would do fine.

On the other hand, Berkeley was one of the best schools in the country—at least that I was likely to be admitted to. Wouldn't it be foolish to pass up a chance to earn my degree there?

I went back and forth all spring trying to make up my mind. In the meantime I decided to enroll in a summer course at Eureka's College of the Redwoods, referred to by irreverent locals as "College of the Retards" or "College of the Deadheads." I'd be able to get a science requirement—not my strong suit— out of the way, and see whether I was really ready for this back to college thing.

I'd also find out how I'd manage living away from the mountain. My friend John Denery, who sang with Brent's TV, the Arcata band renowned for playing shows on street corners, in parking lots, and, most legendarily, in laundromats, was going to be away for the summer. He offered me the use of his apartment, a shabby but homey affair on the low-lying backside of town known as the Bottoms.

It was perfect for my needs. I told John I'd move in as soon as he left, then watched the normally glacial pace of "mountain time" accelerate into overdrive. I had less than a month to prepare for what could turn into an absence of a year or two if I followed this college plan through to completion.

Getting my house and land ready wasn't too hard—I was used to that by now—but in a burst of hubris, folly, or just to demonstrate that Lookout Records was stronger than ever despite David Hayes's departure, I'd set out to release 10 7" EPs in a single month. The same month, it turned out, that I'd be starting my new life in Arcata.

It was the biggest project I'd attempted yet, with or without David. The release date would fall just as classes were starting at CR, and on the day that Redwood Summer was scheduled to kick off with a massive demonstration at the Samoa mill.

Excited as I'd originally been about Redwood Summer, my enthusiasm had been waning. Why, I'm not sure. Maybe I was rebelling because it had become a "big" thing, attracting international support and attention, leaving me far removed from the inner circles of those planning it. Or it could have merely been a case of my historically short attention span, with my monkey mind having already moved on to other things.

I hadn't stopped caring about the trees or the environment. I still recycled, still tried to be a good steward to the land. But I found myself shying away from the level of confrontation that was spreading across the North Coast. When a burly young logger punched 50-year-old protester Mem Hill in the face, breaking her nose, perhaps the most shocking thing was that few people were all that shocked.

Was I turning into a coward? Possibly, but in my heart of hearts I'd always felt like one. I'd been charging haphazardly into gang fights, riots, and political protests since I was a teenager in the 60s, but what others might have seen as courage was more often a combination of foolhardiness and fear of what people might think if I held back.

I loved the look of my Earth First! shirt, with its upraised fist and logo superimposed on a pulsating green background. I was especially proud of it because it had originally belonged to Judi Bari. The first time I saw her wearing it, I'd asked where I could get one.

"I'll trade you," she said. Stripping it off, she stood naked from the waist up, on a Friday afternoon in the middle of downtown Boonville, waiting for me to hand over my tie-dyed hippie shirt in exchange.

But by the time I made it back to Laytonville I'd collected as many dirty looks and muttered comments as I'd gotten in my most-hated days of the early *Lookout* era. I wore the shirt a couple more times with similarly scary results. After that I decided to save it for special occasions, such as when the Lookouts played in logger-free zones like Berkeley or San Francisco.

It wasn't just that I was afraid someone might beat me up—which did feel like a possibility. I also, strange as it might seem, no longer wanted to upset people. I was a serious journalist now, I told myself, a semi-respectable member of the community. Having lived most of my life as an outsider, that felt terribly important.

I was in the middle of moving into John's apartment in Arcata when news came about the bomb that had exploded in Judi Bari's car as she and Darryl Cherney drove through Oakland. I, as well as most people I knew, assumed it had been an assassination attempt. The police and FBI, however, claimed the bomb had actually belonged to Judi and Darryl, and arrested them.

That didn't sound like the Judi and Darryl I knew. But how well, I wondered, did I really know them? In 1969 I'd worked on an organizing project with a beautiful, incredibly charismatic young woman named Diana Oughton. A year later, I saw her face staring back at me from the pages of *Newsweek* after she and two comrades blew themselves up making bombs for the Weather Underground.

While it eventually became obvious, even to the police, that Judi and Darryl were the victims rather than the perpetrators of the bombing, I still felt some of the queasiness and doubt I'd experienced in the wake of the Oughton affair. It wasn't that I blamed them for what had happened, just that, for all my radical bluster, I wasn't ready for things to get quite that serious.

Civil disobedience, maybe even a little sabotage, I could deal with. But people getting blown up? Maybe even me getting blown up? I dashed off an impassioned piece for the *AVA* decrying the Bari bombing and retreated into the cool gray dream world of an Arcata summer.

Spy Rock's unrelenting sunshine became a distant memory. Here, where the mountains flattened out into a broad coastal plain, life unfolded beneath a perennially cloud- and fog-shrouded sky. Regardless of when I passed it, day or night, the Humboldt Bank sign always read 54 degrees. I figured it must be broken, but after a month or two, I realized it was probably telling the truth.

Despite my misgivings in the wake of the bombing, I still planned to take part in Redwood Summer, but on the morning of the first demonstration I woke up feeling like someone had taken a chain saw to my internal organs. By noon I was stretched out on a gurney in the emergency room at Mad River Hospital.

The pain was so intense and overpowering that I was sure I must be dying. Once again, as when I'd been trapped in the snowdrift, I reflected bitterly on how my life was being cut short just as I was finally learning something about how to live.

But it was another false alarm. After a couple hours of tests and scans, the doctors informed me I was "only" suffering from a bad case of kidney stones. "It won't kill you," one said, "though there may be times when the pain has you wishing it would."

He was exaggerating, but not by much. Subsequent attacks brought me back to the hospital on occasion, but injections and pills mostly kept me functional. The more profound effect was psychological. Despite being told I hadn't ever been in real danger, I acted as if I'd been miraculously pulled back from the abyss. I grew determined to wring the most out of however many days, weeks, or decades I had left.

After months of inactivity, the Lookouts got together for what would turn out to be the last time. We played a couple shows and went into the studio to record some songs with Green Day's Billie Joe Armstrong joining us on guitar and backing vocals. It was probably the best work we'd ever done, and also marked the first time that Billie and Tre would play music together.

Green Day toured the country that summer, starting with a hastily thrown together show in the living room of an apartment on 10th Street in Arcata, across from the Greyhound station. Shortly after they got back to California, Al Sobrante, their drummer, announced that he wanted to put the band "on hold" for a couple years while he went away to college.

Billie and Mike, having barely made it out of high school and with no plans for the future other than being in a band, were devastated. Green Day might have died then and there if they hadn't come up with the idea of asking Tre Cool to take Al's place.

As I watched the new lineup play its first show, I knew instantly that the five and a half year story of the Lookouts was over. There had been nothing wrong with Al's drumming, but Tre's talent and skill catapulted Green Day into a new dimension. There was no chance he'd be coming back to us.

Twice in my life there have been summers that passed seamlessly, as if they consisted of a single day and night. One of those was in 1968, the year I first arrived in California. Arcata, 1990, would be the other. Both times I found myself someplace unfamiliar and beguiling; both times my normal worries and restiveness fell away for at least a while, replaced by a pervasive sense of tranquility and wonder.

I commuted to Eureka for classes, did enough homework and study to earn an A, kept up with my Lookout Records and

Lookout magazine responsibilities, and still seemed to have endless amounts of time for making friends, exploring my new town, and, at the age of 42, learning how to skateboard.

With or without my attention, the days and weeks kept ticking away. It came as a shock when John Denery called to remind me he'd need his apartment back soon. I'd put off my decision as long as I could: was I going to find somewhere else to live in Arcata and continue my studies at HSU, or would I be heading south to Berkeley?

In the end, the decision more or less made itself. While I'd procrastinated, dithered, and skated aimlessly through the streets of Arcata, the HSU transfer deadline had come and gone. If I wanted to study there, I'd have to wait at least another semester. Meanwhile, the admissions office at Berkeley called to tell me I was eligible to enroll in classes immediately.

The one remaining obstacle, the lack of somewhere affordable to live, disappeared when my brother offered me the room he'd been using as a workshop for his surfboard business. Three blocks from campus and rent-controlled at 1970s prices, it was too good to pass up, especially since I hadn't been able to find anything nearly as cheap in Arcata.

For all my complaints about not wanting to move to Berkeley, I didn't actively dislike the place. If anything, it was my favorite town in the Bay Area; my reluctance to move back there was more a matter of pride than antipathy. I'd said my goodbyes and become a mountain man; returning, even on a temporary basis, felt like an admission of failure.

But as much as I would miss Arcata's casual, languid ways and the quirky, charming friends I'd met there, fate and the universe were clearly conspiring to send me to Berkeley. And in the end it turned out better than I expected, if a bit unreal at first, like an extended holiday in an educational theme park.

Home still lay high atop Spy Rock, on the hind flanks of Iron Peak, and I was determined not to forget that. In the midst of a less than enthralling lecture, while plowing through some abstruse passage of Marx or Freud, or poring over a record label spread sheet at 3 in the morning, my mind and my heart would go drifting back.

Getting my body there was not as easy. The drive, including a tedious crawl through the ever-expanding suburbs of Marin and Sonoma, took three and a half hours each way. I had so little free time as it was that I resented spending that much of it on Highway 101. More and more often, I found myself saying, "The hell with it, I'll go next week."

The animals would be fine; I had a neighbor looking after them. And though I'd never intended to stay away this much, I assured myself that it was only temporary. Once my degree was finished, I'd be back on Spy Rock for good. I was too busy to notice that life might be making other plans.

There were new friendships and relationships, and an increasing reliance on the conveniences of urban life. Most of all, there was the record label, which continued to grow relentlessly into something bigger and more demanding than I'd ever imagined possible.

By 1991 I had two fulltime employees, a couple dozen bands, and a balance sheet representing more money than I'd ever seen, let alone been responsible for. It was unnerving at times, but the roller coaster was already moving too fast to consider hitting the eject button.

At any rate, the bands and the bills were getting paid, usually with money left over. I guessed—though I didn't like saying or even thinking so out loud for fear of jinxing things—that made it a success.

Trips up north became shorter and less frequent, and

gradually Spy Rock began feeling less familiar. I saw the same people, though not as often, and the same places, but not regularly enough to notice, let alone cherish or rue the inevitable changes. My connection to the land was not yet broken, but it was badly fraying. Instead of making my way back home, I was slowly fading away.

eleven

Udo died in the autumn of 1991. He'd been driving alone late at night, so no one ever knew exactly how his car wound up at the bottom of a ravine. The most likely guess was that he'd swerved to avoid a deer and lost control. We buried him in Little Lake Cemetery at the south end of Willits. Afterward, everyone gathered at Tre's parents' house.

The get-together was one of old mountain friends such as I hadn't seen since the uproarious, carefree parties of the early 80s, albeit with a far more sad and somber purpose. It was hard to avoid noticing an awful symmetry with the day eight and a half years earlier, when, at that same cemetery, we'd buried Udo and Josie's daughter, Kira.

Kira had been an angelic child, who radiated light and cheer wherever she went. Frowns and worries didn't stand a chance in her presence: she'd always find a way to make you laugh or look at things in a brighter, more optimistic way. She was one of those kids who seemed almost preternaturally intelligent and perceptive, the kind of mountain kid who, when I'd first come to Spy Rock, inspired me with such hope for the culture I saw developing there.

The last time I saw Kira was the afternoon she and Bex, Tre's 15-year-old cousin, emerged on horseback from the woods in front of my house. They stopped and chatted, I snapped a blurry photo, and they rode on down the hill in the direction of Tre's house. A week or two later, she collapsed in her classroom at Willits High, and died almost instantly from an aneurysm. She was 16.

It was spring, well into April already, the day we buried her, but a harsh, chilly breeze tossed clouds across a dismal, tattered sky. As they lowered her coffin, Udo all but flung himself into the grave, his coat flapping in the wind as he cried, "My baby, my darling baby!" It was a shocking moment, made all the more startling because Udo, a strong, stoic man, was almost never given to overt displays of emotion.

When I first came to Spy Rock, I'd been searching for something more "real" than the hothouse existence of city life. "A man could die up here if he wasn't careful," I remembered thinking.

The idea of death being a more constant and palpable presence in the mountains was probably not accurate—no doubt people die with similar frequency and drama wherever you are—but it felt that way. The difference, I think, is that in the city, you seldom know more than a handful of your immediate neighbors, whereas in the country you're aware of, if not directly affected by, every death that happens for miles around.

And though Kira's and Udo's deaths hit closest to home, there were others. Many others. Michael Ferretta dropped dead of a heart attack, Judi Bari passed away from cancer. Teepee Doug, spokesperson for the ragtag band of hippies who'd tried to frighten me out of the publishing business, spun out of control on the sharp curve where 101 shifts from Sonoma freeway to Mendocino highway. Lester, who lived just over the creek from me, and Craig, his younger brother, both had their hearts give out while still in their 40s.

Not to mention the slow but steady stream of accidents and murders that, while they might involve strangers or people known only by name or reputation, cast a pall over the land. There was the woman, for example, whose mangled remains were found in a streambed near Registered Guest Road, a mile beyond the Iron Peak turnoff.

It was clear to investigators that a bear had eaten her; what remained a mystery was whether the bear had killed her, or merely happened upon her body after she had died from other causes. People were inclined—or preferred—to believe the latter. The number of bears roaming the woods had increased noticeably since the 80s, and it was unsettling to think any of them might be preying specifically on humans.

Udo's funeral was the first time I'd seen Tre since the previous summer. He'd been spending nearly all his time on tour with Green Day, who were now attracting attention from far beyond the punk rock scene. Frank, Tre's dad, told us about his plan to refurbish an old bookmobile and turn it into a tour van so he could drive the band around, something he would wind up doing right on through their major label breakthrough in 1994.

Even in late 1991, it was obvious that the band was headed for much bigger things, and everybody had an opinion about what their next step should be. Frank had been telling Tre ever since he joined the Lookouts that he needed to get "on a big label like Warner Brothers."

I first heard him deliver that opinion while watching a video of his beloved ZZ Top, who—coincidentally enough—were on Warner, and who Frank regularly cited as his idea of a band who were "doing it right." But he was only one of many people saying it was time Green Day moved to a "real" label.

This always exasperated me. I couldn't see what made Lookout anything less than real. I felt we'd been doing—and were continuing to do—a pretty good job taking care of Green Day's interests. Their records were selling in the tens of thousands, and they were getting paid a better percentage than they would have at almost any label, major or independent.

Between record sales and touring, Green Day had become all but self-sufficient.

In January of 1992, their second album sold out its entire pressing of 10,000 copies the day it was released, and we—by underground standards, anyway—had a hit on our hands. Combined with the success of Operation Ivy and the first Green Day album, it meant Lookout Records was generating more income than I had ever earned in my life.

Hardly something to complain about, you'd think, but immersed as I was in trying to finish my senior thesis and graduate from Berkeley, it was like finding myself astride the proverbial tiger. Not that I was in any hurry to dismount; releasing punk rock records was proving to be more fun than I was likely to have trying to control classrooms of unruly high school students. The pay was better, too.

But substitute teaching had been a central part of my plan for returning to Spy Rock. As it became obvious that I neither wanted to nor could afford to abandon my responsibilities as a newly minted record mogul, the Spy Rock dream slipped further from my grasp.

First months, then years, went by without progress toward moving back to the mountain. It would have been easy enough—especially after Green Day's meteoric rise to superstardom in 1994 sent our grosses from the hundreds of thousands into the millions—to refit and rewire the Spy Rock house so I could run the label from there. Instead, I found myself preferring to let it remain a telephone and internet-free escape hatch for when the pressures of business grew too overwhelming.

My visits seldom lasted more than a few days; sometimes I'd drive there and back in a single day, spending more time on the road than at the house. But in mid-September of 1993, a relationship gone sour combined with the ever-mounting demands of keeping Lookout on an even keel left me on the brink of a mental meltdown. It was agreed—my employees being especially vocal on the subject—that I needed some time off.

I spent the first several days at Spy Rock, sleeping, playing with the animals, and ruefully taking inventory of the repairs and maintenance I'd been neglecting. Then I set off on a rambling journey through the bleak wilds of Northeastern California, and on into Oregon, Idaho, Montana, Alberta, and British Columbia. The scenery, the weather, everything was heartbreakingly, exquisitely, last-breath-of-summer beautiful until I reached Vancouver. Then a bank of clouds lurched in from the sea, bearing the first of the chilly autumn rains.

I knew it was time to go, and drove the 835 miles back to Spy Rock in a single maniacal dash. Summer hadn't fully faded from the sun-dappled California hills; the soft, warm air caressed my face as I rounded the last bend and started up the driveway. Kong greeted me in the usual spot, but not Ruf-Ruf. Odd, I thought; except for the time when she'd been bitten by the snake, she'd always been there to welcome me home.

As I drove the rest of the way down to the house, I could see her sleeping under the wind chime and crystal-laden Ponderosa pine that had grown from infancy to hold pride of place in what could loosely be termed the front yard. She wasn't as young as she used to be, and her frenetically paced running and barking had noticeably slowed over the past couple years.

But old or not, she would practically turn herself inside out with excitement, barely able to stay on two feet, let alone four, when she saw me pulling in after a long absence. It was almost unthinkable that she'd sleep right through my arrival. It wasn't until I got out of the car and walked over to where she lay that I realized she wasn't sleeping.

I loved both dogs, but Ruf-Ruf had always been the special one. She knew it, and made sure Kong did, too, nipping and yelping at him when he got in her way, though she was barely half his size. Living in the mountains had made me aware of nature's darker side, but even so, I wasn't prepared for Kong's reaction to the death of his longtime companion and sometime tormenter.

Within hours after I buried Ruf-Ruf, Kong had dug her up and begun systematically demolishing her corpse. I didn't personally witness him doing this, but it looked suspiciously like he'd made a meal or two out of it.

I buried her again, this time covering the grave with heavy stones, but by morning he'd managed to dig her up again. The cats and I watched as he snarlingly ripped tufts of blond fur from her tattered hide. He'd been holding back these feelings for a long time, apparently.

Ruf-Ruf's death left a huge void, irretrievably altering the Spy Rock chemistry. Kong kept close to me whenever I was around, begging openly for the attention Ruf-Ruf had always had first dibs on, but he lacked the unbridled exuberance she had brought to the simplest stroll around the land.

The cats continued to lead separate and aloof existences, disappearing for days or weeks to prowl the forests or... who knew, really, where they went or what they got up to? I often gave them up for lost and presumed eaten.

But time and again one or more of them would turn up bedraggled and mewling beneath my window on some random dawn, missing bits of fur, bearing mysterious bite marks, yet eager to return to the comforts of home and a regularly refilled food tray, purring and playful as ever. Then, just like that, they'd vanish again into the wild.

Ruf-Ruf had been the anchor that kept the animal family together, even during my long absences. Once she was gone, the cats, who as kittens often spent cold nights cuddled with her in the doghouse, came around far less frequently. Sometimes during my visits now, I wouldn't see them at all.

And they were just visits, that was the saddest thing. In 1985, after the first Lookouts show, when I seemed to be at war with half the mountain, Indiana Slim had described me as a salmon swimming upstream. He could have been looking into the future and seeing my attempts to find my way back to a home that was no longer there.

1996 marked my last serious stab at living on the mountain. With Lookout having moved into a suite of offices and accumulated a staff of 14 employees, it was no longer a big deal for me to let things run on their own for a while as I attempted to re-establish myself on Spy Rock.

I made several tries, and they always ran something like this: arriving late in the afternoon, I'd examine the premises, and make a list of everything that had to be repaired or replaced. In the morning I'd drive to Laytonville or Willits to buy the necessary materials, but by the time I got back from town I'd be too tired to do anything more that day.

Or the next day, or the day after, as it typically turned out. The pressures and responsibilities of running Lookout had left me so exhausted that, once swallowed up by the hypnotic stillness of Spy Rock, I mostly dozed fitfully on the sofa and reflected on the chaotic whirlwind of activity my city life had become.

One brisk, intermittently rainy afternoon, I was lying there in my usual position, my eyes opening every so often to take in the lush array of spring greenery that looked intent on overrunning the mountainside. In the midst of this reverie, I was jolted wide awake by the sight of a large black dog strolling past my window.

It wasn't common, but nor was it unheard of, for strange dogs to come sniffing around. Usually it would be a neighbor's animal in search of adventure, companionship, or a better quality of food than it was getting at home.

But you couldn't let them make a habit of it; otherwise, you'd wind up feeding half the cats and dogs on the mountain. So I stepped outside to shoo the visitor away, wondering who it could belong to. Apart from Kong, I wasn't aware of any other black dogs in the area.

This one was at least twice the size of Kong, who, strangely, had disappeared, and who I later found cowering at the top of the driveway. I came almost close enough to reach out and pet the interloper before realizing it was not a dog at all, but a young black bear.

"Go on," I shouted, "get out of here! Shoo! No bears here! Only people, dogs, and cats!"

He looked at me quizzically, as if I'd hurt his feelings, then, with a slightly insolent shrug, padded off into the forest. A couple days later he was back. This time he wasn't as ready to leave when I asked him to. I wound up having to bang on a pot with a large spoon to emphasize my point.

It was the beginning of an almost year-long contest of wills. Captain Ahab had his white whale, I had my black bear, and in both cases, the animal kingdom seemed to be winning.

If I was at home when he showed up, I could chase him off, but each time it got harder. He'd figured out that my yelling and noisemaking had no power to hurt him, and also seemed to understand that sooner or later I'd be leaving again. As soon as I did, he'd move in and make himself at home.

Having found the spot under the house where I left food for Kong and the cats, he'd scarf down a week's supply in a single sitting, then spend the next day or two sleeping. My animals were left hungry and out in the cold. As he matured into a full-grown bear, he saw no point in waiting for me to come back and refill the food trays.

He tore the padlocked door off the shed and devoured everything inside, including 100 pounds of dog food and three bags of fertilizer. Then he turned his attention to the front door of my house, leaving it riddled with claw marks, though he didn't manage to get in.

At least not this time. But his intentions were clear. He'd lost all fear of me; shouting, pot-banging, rock-throwing—none of it worked anymore. He'd just look back at me as if I were a mildly annoying idiot. The only way I could chase him off now was with a blast or two from the shotgun. I shot in the air, not at him, but even that seemed to be losing its effectiveness. I wondered if more drastic measures might become necessary.

They did. I came home one afternoon to find the back window shattered and my kitchen in ruins. It looked as though the bear had been poking around on the back deck, stood up on his hind legs to peer in the window, and fallen through it into the house. Once inside, he'd smashed open everything that looked remotely like food, leaving a trail of broken glass and molasses in his wake as he headed over to the living room sofa for a nap.

People accuse me of making up the part about the nap, but the evidence was clear: a deep depression in the cushions where he'd been lying, and a blanket covered with burrs and bits of fur. After resting a while, he'd made his exit by pushing out a window screen on the side porch, leaving a couple more claw marks as his calling card.

It took the rest of the day to clean up the mess. Because he'd shattered not just the glass, but the entire window frame, the only repair I could manage was to cover it with polyethylene sheeting—hippie glass, we sometimes called it. I slept uneasily, assuming he'd be back. It was only a question of when.

Until then I hadn't seriously considered shooting him. Partly because I was supposedly a nonviolent vegetarian, partly because the idea just plain terrified me. What if I missed, or only wounded him? What if the gun misfired or jammed just as he came charging at me?

Even if I did manage to kill him, what would I do with a 300-pound corpse? I had no idea how I'd bury something that big, but I couldn't just leave it in my front yard to rot. Not to mention, though it was far from my first concern, that shooting bears out of season and without a license was highly illegal.

What choice did I have, though? Either the bear had to go or I did. Worried I'd arrive home one day to find him in the house again, I began taking the shotgun with me whenever I left the mountain.

It had been years since I'd been stopped by the police, let alone been given a ticket. But one of the first times I drove to the city with the shotgun in my trunk, the legendary CHP officer known to everyone up and down Highway 101 simply as "Clarence" pulled me over midway between Laytonville and Willits.

As was his usual MO, Clarence claimed he smelled marijuana and asked to search my car. He'd been using that ruse for years and had single-handedly busted hundreds of people transporting pot to the city. In my case, however, I knew he was straight-up lying. I was driving a brand new car, one that had never carried or had the slightest contact with marijuana.

I hadn't even smoked marijuana since 1993, when a couple tokes had triggered a crippling panic attack during my trip through the Canadian Rockies. So while I understood that

Clarence had a job to do, I didn't appreciate him being brazenly dishonest with me, and told him so.

"I can't search your car without permission," he allowed. "But if you'd prefer to do this the hard way, we can sit here for a few hours while we wait for a canine team to get here from Ukiah and give the car a going-over. They're very thorough. You never know what they'll find."

Was he threatening me? Despite all the hippie paranoia floating around, I'd never believed the cops would go so far as to plant evidence in people's cars, especially when there were so many real traffickers to be caught. At the same time, I knew they could get away with it if they wanted to. The cops' word against that of a guy driving down from Spy Rock? Even I'd be inclined to believe the cops.

Regardless of whether I could trust the police not to frame me, I didn't want to spend the rest of the afternoon sitting on the side of the road. So, much as it pained me, I opened the trunk for Officer Clarence to have a look. The first thing he saw, of course, was my (thankfully unloaded) shotgun.

If it had been loaded, I would have been in some trouble. Clarence gave me a stern lecture about the legal way to transport weapons, with the gun kept in a separate part of the vehicle from the ammo. At the same time, he seemed to grow a little more deferential toward me, as if carrying a gun made me more respectable than your average Spy Rocker.

My next encounter with the police didn't go that smoothly. This time I was driving my old Subaru station wagon, so it wasn't possible to keep shotgun and ammo separated. I compensated as best as I could by stashing the gun at the back of the car and the ammo in the glove box.

While I won't claim to be someone who never broke a traffic law, I usually did so judiciously enough not to get caught.

There was nothing judicious, however, about my driving that night. Riled up about something at Lookout, I was anxious to get back to the office to set it right. Near the Marin-Sonoma line I encountered a car that insisted on poking along at 45 mph in the fast lane.

I blinked my lights, honked my horn, tailgated him, but he wouldn't move over. When I tried passing him on the right he would speed up so I couldn't get around him; then, as soon as I got stuck behind traffic in the right lane, he'd slow back down to 45. Whatever his reasons, he seemed determined to make sure I wouldn't get to the city before he did.

After half an hour of this, I was beside myself with rage, all but literally frothing at the mouth. When I saw red lights flashing behind me, my reaction was one of exuberance. It's rare you see someone get pulled over for deliberately obstructing traffic, but it looked like this time justice was going to be done. Imagine my surprise, then, when the cop directed me to the side of the road.

"Why are you stopping me?" I demanded. "That guy in front of me is crazy! You need to get him off the road before he causes an accident!"

"With all due respect, sir," the officer said, "you were the one who looked crazy." If I'd been slightly less agitated, I might have seen his point. But I was too busy being outraged that the driver causing me such misery was getting away with it while I, a sane and responsible citizen, was being unjustly detained.

My troubles were only beginning. When a police officer asks if you have any weapons in the vehicle, you ideally want to be able to tell him calmly, coolly, and truthfully that no, in fact you do not. Unfortunately in my case, this was not possible. Assuming that things would go better if I told him the simple, unvarnished truth, I did, and was surprised to find myself shoved up against the side of the car and handcuffed.

I'd been in this position before—quite a few times, actually, during my hippie and greaser days—but with a couple decades having passed since the last time it happened, I was out of practice. Once I'd calmed down, though, the cop turned out to be not such a bad guy after all.

After discovering that the shotgun wasn't loaded and that I wasn't quite as much of a lunatic as I'd first appeared, he took off the handcuffs and let me sit on the hood of his car while he finished searching mine. He wasn't taking any chances, though.

"Just so you know, if you budge from that spot, I'll be justified in opening fire," he said matter-of-factly.

Shivering in a cold wind and gradually coming back to my senses, I sat there for about 20 minutes while he gave my car a thorough going-over. The cop and I wound up having a nice chat before he let me go without even giving me a ticket. But clearly this bear business was weighing too heavily on my nerves and needed to be brought to a conclusion.

On my return to the mountain, and with a full moon coming up, I decided to lay a trap. I filled an old cooking pot—already sporting a couple bullet holes from a previous encounter with a pesky raccoon—with dog food and set it in front of the house, in plain view of my upstairs bedroom window.

The shotgun lay beside my bed, loaded with one-ounce lead slugs that were supposedly capable of blasting a hole several inches wide in almost anything they hit. I'd slept that way since the bear's first home invasion, but tonight I had no intention of sleeping.

Based on his usual behavior, I expected the bear would turn up sometime around midnight. Lying on my back in an adrenaline-charged state of combat readiness, I never imagined

I'd have trouble staying awake, but somehow I drifted off. I found myself standing on the shore of a semi-circular bay, at the center of which lay an island that looked like a cross between San Francisco and Normandy's Mont St. Michel.

Water lapped at my feet; fish, dolphins, and eels splashed and leapt about. Then came a great sucking sound, as if someone had removed the plug from a bathtub. The water rushed away as it might ahead of a tsunami, leaving a vast expanse of sand covered with plastic inflatable sea creatures in pretty pastel colors. The one I remember most vividly was a dead ringer for an old-fashioned cream-and-green Checker cab.

Before I had time to make sense of this spectacle, the water came roaring back. Just as the sea was about to wash me away, I awoke, sat up straight, heart pounding and nerves pumping a double blast of electricity to my fingertips. I knew without having to look that the bear was here.

Sliding across the bed, shotgun in hand, I peered out the window. There he was, halfway through the pot of dog food. Leaning back on his haunches, he looked so harmless and playful that I felt a twinge of guilt for tricking him this way. I had to force myself to recall the havoc he'd been wreaking on my life.

Although the gun held eight rounds, I knew it was the first shot that would count. If I didn't bring him down with that one, there was no telling what might happen. But at this range—no more than 20 feet—how could I miss?

During my years on the mountain I'd shot skunks, raccoons, rattlesnakes, even a few obstreperous blue jays— don't ask—but I'd never imagined coming up against anything this much bigger and stronger than me. What did I think I was doing? Couldn't I just give up, retreat to Berkeley, and let the bear have its way?

That's what my city friends had been telling me to do. They were horrified when I mentioned the possibility of shooting it. "He's just doing what bears do," they protested. "It's his home. You're the one that's trespassing."

That line of reasoning irritated the hell out of me. "I was living on that land years before that bear came around, before he was even born," I argued. "And his home is a hole in the ground out in the woods. I don't go poking around in his den, and all I'm asking is that he stay out of mine."

City people seemed to picture my land as some sort of Jellystone Park, with me as the villain trying to stymie the jolly, fun-loving, picnic basket-stealing bear. "If you won't share your land with him, at least call the rangers and have them move him somewhere where he'll be happy," they'd say. No one wanted to believe me when I told them this was neither a cartoon nor the Discovery Channel, and that up on Spy Rock there weren't any "rangers" to take care of bear problems.

These thoughts and conversations raced through my mind as I picked out my target and prepared to fire. I thought about aiming for his head, but it made more sense to go for the heart. The head would be too easy to miss, whereas I only had to hit him somewhere in the vicinity of the heart to stop him.

Struggling to get my breath under control, I reminded myself one last time to squeeze rather than pull the trigger. But at the crucial moment my concentration broke, my arm jerked slightly, and though a deafening explosion rang out across the canyon, the bear didn't fall. Instead, he jerked spasmodically, his hindquarters lurching into the air. After the briefest of pauses, he went tearing off at breakneck speed down the hill, into the woods and out of sight.

I must have hit him somewhere; he was too big a target to have missed entirely. But it made no sense that a wounded animal could move that fast. And when I examined the area the following morning, there was not a trace of blood or fur to be found.

Whether he'd been hurt or not, he never came near the house again. Some months later he gave me a scare when I ran into him in the woods at the bottom of the hill. I wasn't carrying a weapon and was completely defenseless, but he took one look at me and ran away.

Having vanquished, or at least banished, my black beast, I began drifting away from the land again. So, too, did my animals; the last of the cats disappeared for good, and only Kong remained. Now that I no longer had to worry about the bear stealing his food, I could leave enough to last him a month or more at a time. I felt bad thinking about Kong wandering around alone up there, but still couldn't find time to visit more often.

One chilly February evening I realized it had been too long—less than a month, true, but in winter it was more important to keep the food supply replenished, since I never knew when I might get snowed out. On the spur of the moment I grabbed my pal Robert Eggplant and took a late night dash up to the mountain, stopping at the Willits Safeway for a couple 50-pound bags of dog food.

There wasn't much snow on the roads, but a lot of frost, the crystals sparkling and shimmering in the glow of my high beams. I could hear and feel the ground crunching beneath my wheels as I pulled into the driveway. Just after rounding the bend above the house, I ran over a rock or a log that, as often happened in winter, had most likely fallen onto the road from the hillside above.

It was enough of a bump that I thought I'd better check to see if it had done any damage, but figured I'd wait until I got down to the house. Kong was nowhere to be seen, which was unlike him. In all the years he'd lived there, I'd never known him to wander out of hailing distance.

With a sinking feeling, I remembered the bump in the road, and walked back up the driveway to find Kong's corpse, frozen so solid that my car hadn't put a dent in it. If there was any consolation, I found plenty of food left under the house, so at least I knew he hadn't starved to death.

He'd been showing his age for a while; 12 years isn't a long lifespan for a city dog, but mountain life tends to be a bit harder on both animals and people. Ruf-Ruf had been the same age when she'd given up the ghost.

I got out my guitar and played a memorial song. Lacking anything in my repertoire about deceased dogs, I sang "Sam's Song," a number I'd written for my new band, the Potatomen, about the sad and lonely streets of Eureka. The ground was frozen too hard to dig him a proper grave, but the following day a blizzard swept in and left him buried beneath the snow until spring.

twelve

With no more animals to look after, my visits to Spy Rock grew still less frequent. Meanwhile, Lookout Records was reaching what would prove to be its zenith, with sales in the millions of dollars and a roster of bands hailing from across the USA, Canada, and the UK.

It was important to keep in touch with the bands, attend their shows when possible, and be available to answer questions and lend moral support. That didn't necessarily require me to be constantly traveling, at least not as much as I wound up doing, but it was something I came to enjoy.

I knew the bands appreciated seeing me in the audience and hanging out with them backstage instead of being some anonymous guy in an office thousands of miles away. But it meant being away from home—whether "home" meant Berkeley or Spy Rock—much of the time. When I wasn't out visiting or working with other bands, I'd often be touring, or recording or rehearsing, with my own.

When the ever mounting demands of the record industry threatened to overwhelm me, I would retreat not to Spy Rock, but to London, where Olivia always kept a spare room waiting. During one such visit, shortly after the bear saga concluded, she blurted out that she was in danger of losing her apartment because her old age pension was no longer enough to cover the upkeep and taxes.

Olivia always tried to put the best face on things, and was openly contemptuous of people she called "moaning Minnies."

But she couldn't hide how unhappy she was at the prospect of having to sell the place and, as she put it, "live out the rest of my days in some grotty little basement in the suburbs."

British property values were deeply depressed at the time, having not yet recovered from the recession of the early 90s, so selling the flat wouldn't net her anywhere near what it had once been worth. But she couldn't afford to sit there waiting for prices to rise, so she'd already accepted an almost insultingly low offer from a real estate speculator. By the time she'd paid off her mortgage, she'd have barely enough left to live on.

"Don't sell it to that guy. I'll buy it, and then you can keep on living here," I told her, barely stopping to think about what I was saying. It was a near-replay of the spur-of-the-moment decision-making that had led to my buying the house on Spy Rock. Apart from helping Olivia and ensuring I'd still have a place to stay when visiting London, it made no sense at all.

I already felt overburdened by a house and land I couldn't find time to look after, and a job that seemed to grow more demanding every day. Certain bands, and people I worked with, too, had been making noises to the effect that I was out of the office too much as it was. What did I think I was going to do with an apartment 6,000 miles away in London?

In the weeks and months that followed, though, the method behind my apparent madness began to reveal itself. For at least a year, probably longer, I'd been growing dissatisfied with Lookout Records and my role there. Despite the label's astonishing success—a success that enabled me to do things like, well, casually buy apartments in London—I'd grown sick of it and wanted out.

London came to represent for me what Spy Rock once had: a peaceful refuge from what had started out as a carefree, goofball, punk rock adventure, but now felt way too much like a generic high-stress office job. In 1995, I published—six months late—the tenth-anniversary issue of *Lookout* magazine, never dreaming it would also be the last. I just couldn't find time anymore to do the writing that had once been my main creative outlet.

I still had my music, but it was getting harder and harder to fit Potatomen shows and practices into an ever more frenetic work schedule. I caught myself resenting the fact that I'd spent the last ten years helping other musicians and artists while neglecting so many of my own ambitions.

In the spring of 1997 I flipped out—or, depending how you looked at it, made a rational and necessary decision. With approximately one day's notice, I resigned my position at Lookout Records and essentially gave away the company I had spent the last ten years building. Though not fully realizing it at the time, I was also walking away from millions of dollars and setting in motion the circumstances that would ultimately lead to the label's demise.

Out of a lifetime of crazy and self-destructive decisions, this one might have taken the cake, but at that moment I was so mentally and emotionally shattered that I didn't know what else to do. For the first few days after I cleaned out my desk, I was like a man who'd had a limb or two amputated, still in shock, still not fully grasping what had happened.

But, I kept telling myself, I was free! Free to go anywhere, free to do anything I wanted. A perfect time, you might think, to finally go back home to Spy Rock. Instead I headed straight for London, where I was to spend most of the next 10 years.

I visited California often enough, but seeing friends and family usually took precedence over Spy Rock. When I did manage to drag myself back up the mountain, I seldom stayed more than a day or two, just long enough to sadly survey the rack and ruin into which my once beautiful home was falling.

The land, on the other hand, was flourishing. Trees had grown taller, the forest canopy thicker. Once-barren hillsides had been colonized by hardy manzanitas staking out a habitat for the oaks, firs, and pines that would follow. But while nature was thriving and unfolding in its own untroubled way, my feeble efforts hadn't fared so well.

The grapevines were dead, victims of insufficient water and a series of killer frosts. A similar fate had befallen the plum and nectarine trees, and most of the raspberries and strawberries. Some of the hardier herbs had done better: thyme, rosemary, and sage grew wildly on the north side of the house, and an ever-spreading lavender bush scattered its fragrance for hundreds of yards around.

The fields of crimson clover had lost their vitality, but still dazzled briefly every spring. They paled, though, in comparison with the daffodils I had whimsically planted in sunny spots all across the land and which had multiplied and spread until whole hillsides pulsated in symphonies of yellow. Two spindly cherry trees hung on—barely—but my apple tree, the one I'd spent two days smashing and hauling away rock to make room for, now dominated a once barren hillside.

Of the hundreds of pine and fir seedlings I'd planted on the north slope, only two had survived, but they stood strong, stately and majestic, twin sentinels over the entrance to the land. Barring forest fires or the odd volcanic eruption, they'd occupy that ground for centuries.

I was proud of having kept my promise to protect the land against the logger's axe and the developer's bulldozer, but ashamed at having let so much of my own work slip away. A self-perpetuating downward spiral ensued: I'd return for a visit, full of idealistic plans to whip things back into shape, but confronted with the magnitude of the task, would grow so discouraged that I'd stay away even longer.

As the earth clawed back the little niche I'd carved out of the wilderness, civilization came closing in as well. Where once I could wander across my land and hundreds of adjoining acres without seeing or hearing a sign that other human beings existed, there now remained only a handful of spots where I wouldn't be reminded of—and sometimes disturbed by—my increasingly numerous neighbors.

The woman who owned the land above mine—her property line came within a stone's throw or two of my front door—had in years past rarely put in more than an annual appearance for a long summer weekend. But now she was spending months at a time up there, and talking about building a year-round house. Worse, she wanted permission to run a road across my property to gain access to her building site.

The sliver of land she wanted to use wasn't a problem, but the route of her proposed road was: it would have cars—no telling how many or how often—passing within a hundred yards of my door. I told her as nicely as possible that I couldn't let her do that, only to discover that in my absence she'd cut down several trees on my property and begun laying out her road anyway.

The fact that we'd gotten along well in the past didn't help at all. If anything, it made matters worse. She knew I was away most of the time, and we both knew that once she'd built the road and begun using it, there wouldn't be much I could do about it unless I wanted to spend the next few years hanging around the Mendocino County Courthouse filing lawsuits.

The solution I hit upon was to park one of my junk cars— like many country dwellers, I'd accumulated a few over the years—across the disputed strip of land. She was furious, but the spot she needed to get through was so narrow, bounded by a stream on one side and a cliff on the other, that with the car sitting where I'd left it, her road had nowhere to go.

I'd won that round, but still felt uneasy. In such an isolated setting, the last thing I needed was a neighbor who was not only mad at me, but was also aware of when I was and wasn't around. And while I knew I was within my rights, I couldn't help feeling I was being less than, well, neighborly. We continued to exchange nasty words and dirty looks for some time afterward, but otherwise the situation remained a stalemate.

Then one day I came back to find my driveway sealed off by a metal gate. I was locked out of my own land. Heavy-duty gates had long been *de rigueur* in those parts, of course, but I'd always resisted installing one. There'd once been a metal cable, strung between two trees, that furnished some protection (until you figured out that with some effort you could squeeze a small car under it). But eventually I'd grown tired of locking and unlocking the thing, so for years there'd been nothing to stop anyone from driving right up to my door.

Where could this new gate have come from? Had squatters taken over my land while I was away? Had the property been seized by the sheriff because I'd forgotten to pay my taxes? Was the woman up the hill exacting some weird sort of revenge?

As it turned out, the gate had been put in by yet another new neighbor. He'd bought the property just below mine and, thanks to a long-standing but little-noticed provision in my deed, had also acquired the right to use my driveway as an access road.

He was clearly planning on making full use of that right. Besides installing the gate, he'd trucked in multiple loads of gravel and graded the road until, by mountain standards, it resembled a superhighway. He was building a new house, where he was planning to live fulltime, and had excavated what was once a barely visible watering hole, turning it into a full-fledged lake, complete with dock and boat.

That broad expanse of water should have been a cheering sight, especially set against the parched and sun-baked hills of late summer. If it had been on my own property, I'm sure it would have. Instead, it served as a not quite galling, but definitely annoying reminder that I was no longer master of all I surveyed.

While I missed the days of complete solitude, the gate did provide a sense of security during my long absences. So did having someone living nearby enough to notice any strangers snooping around. It had been more than a decade since I'd had a working lock on my front door, or felt a need to have one, but it felt as though times might be changing.

Maybe being away so much was making me paranoid, but I'd been hearing stories about burglaries and even violent home invasions. I still didn't really worry about it until the day I came home to find that someone—or several someones—had been in the house, helped themselves to some food and beer, and departed with a few tools and utensils.

I felt sick to my stomach, not to mention frightened and helpless. Now that whoever it was had discovered what easy pickings were to be had, surely it was only a matter of time before they'd be back to clean out the rest of the house.

I was enormously relieved to learn that the "burglar" was actually my sister, who was still living on the other side of the mountain and had fallen on hard times. Hard enough, she reasoned—I can't say I blamed her—to justify helping herself to my house and its contents, now that I'd all but abandoned it.

She'd been enduring a hellish several years. Jeff, my brother-in-common-law, had devolved from comical pothead to oafish bully. After subjecting her and her two older children to years of physical and emotional abuse, he'd finally left for good, taking the two younger boys with him.

With Jethro and Gabrielle having grown up and moved away, she was completely on her own, eking out a meager existence in a half-finished cabin without electricity or running water. I found her, on one of the first really cold days of winter, wandering around trying to pick up enough small sticks—she didn't own a saw—to keep a fire going in her stove.

The home she and Jeff had once shared, where I'd stayed during my first visits to Spy Rock in 1980, was gone. Literally. After years of remodeling and rebuilding saw that once-humble structure morph into a slightly lopsided four-story glass and redwood palace, Jeff had grown bored or frustrated with how the redesign was going, hired a bulldozer, and pushed the whole house over the side of the hill.

That folly alone must have cost him hundreds of thousands of dollars, but he still had plenty of money to hire lawyers and hound my sister through the courts for more than a decade after they separated. Not satisfied with gaining full custody of their sons, he then set about trying to strip her of the cabin and land that were her sole remaining assets.

Assisting him in this bitter quest was a well-connected—and expensive—Garberville lawyer more commonly known for his dedication to the environment and civil rights ("civil rights," in those parts, usually meaning the right to grow marijuana without going to prison for it).

The rest of the family did what we could, but my sister was a gentle and vulnerable person, sometimes too trusting for her own good, and not well-suited to the rough-and-tumble of courtroom battles. She was hopelessly unprepared for her ex-partner's scorched earth, take-no-prisoners tactics.

It was not my first time observing Emerald Triangle-style justice in action—I'd covered several trials for the *AVA* and the *Lookout*—but the pervasive corruption and callousness was breathtaking nonetheless. I was especially fascinated by the way the professional classes that enriched themselves from cases like this—judges, lawyers, social workers, therapists, and the like—studiously ignored the fact that this brutal vendetta was being underwritten—as was, for that matter, the North Coast's entire economy—by illegal drug money.

There'd been a time when Big Timber completely dominated the region; anything or anyone that impeded the free flow of logs and lumber would be left on the side of the road with skid marks on its back. But with most of the trees—the loggable ones, anyway—gone now, Big Marijuana had taken over.

It was a case of being careful what you wished for. In the 80s and early 90s, I'd been a vocal cheerleader for the benefits produced by the marijuana trade: the alternative and countercultural institutions it subsidized, the way it had turned a poverty-stricken backwater into a land of burgeoning opportunity.

But an economy or culture that depends on institutionalized illegality risks becoming cynical, corrupt, and squalid. Critics argued that the Emerald Triangle had come to resemble a drug-producing banana republic. I was no longer inclined to disagree.

On a plot of land not far down the road from me, a warren of trashed cars and machinery had sprung up, populated by near-feral mountain kids. I knew some of them by name or sight, or had once known their parents. With little in the way of education, ill equipped for life away from the mountain, they tore about on dirt bikes and—so the stories went—crossbred their dogs with wolves.

Like many of the best mountain tales, the one about the wolf-dogs may have been exaggerated or just plain made up. But the fact that I was willing to consider it possibly being true gave me pause. I wondered if I still belonged here at all.

I'd been kicking the question around for years, but now the answer began to feel painfully clear: there was no longer a future for me on Spy Rock. I was more at home in London—or, for that matter, New York, where I'd recently begun spending time. I wasn't sure if mountain life had genuinely grown darker, or if it merely seemed that way because I was observing it from a distance. Either way, I no longer felt equipped to deal with it.

Still I procrastinated. Another year or two slipped away. Then came the day when I found all the windows shot out of my once pristine but now defunct 1967 Ford pickup. The thought of people wandering around my property random-ly shooting at things was chilling. It left me no longer in any doubt that it was time to go.

Spent shotgun shells lay scattered along the driveway, some only steps from my front door. The house was undam-aged, and showed no sign of having been entered, but the protective spell, the near-enchantment I'd always imagined hanging over the land, was irrevocably broken.

I set aside several weeks in the summer of 2004 to do what had to be done. It would be the longest time I'd spent on Spy Rock since the 1990s. Several derelict vehicles needed to be hauled out, and 22 years worth of tools, treasures, and trash had to be moved, sold, given away, or otherwise disposed of.

When I'd first moved to the mountains, I thought that to fit in I had to drive a cartoonishly crappy old truck. I'd most likely gotten the idea from the place I got most of my ideas about country life: watching *Green Acres* and *The Dukes of Hazzard*. A week before arriving on Spy Rock in 1982, I spent an exorbitant $600 on a barely functioning '63 Chevy pickup.

Trailing great, malevolent clouds of blue-black smoke, it had limped up Highway 101 and over the last few miles of mountain roads to my front door, where it promptly expired, never to run again. Before realizing the truck's condition was terminal, Anne and I had filled it with bottles, cans, and trash that I was going to take to the Laytonville dump "one of these days."

Over the years the forest had grown up around the forlorn vehicle. It looked in danger of being swallowed by the earth, which had already reached the top of its wheel wells. The man from the Laytonville junkyard said he'd be happy to take it off my hands—for a fee of course—but not until I'd emptied it of the morass of cans, disintegrated garbage bags, long-dead yogurt containers, and the innumerable shards of broken glass to which hundreds of bottles had mysteriously reduced themselves.

I was disconsolately sifting and shoveling my way through the rubble when I encountered a cute little lizard sitting defiantly astride a rusty can. Bright green in color, maybe four or five inches long, it bore an uncanny resemblance to a miniature dinosaur. As I drew nearer to investigate, it reared back on its hind legs and hissed menacingly at me.

"There, there, little fellow," I chuckled. "I know it's a nuisance, but you're not going to be able to live here anymore." I gave the top of his head a reassuring pat with my fingertip. He responded by sinking his surprisingly sharp teeth into my finger and refusing to let go.

I had to violently swing my hand back and forth half a dozen times before managing to shake him loose. Even after he'd hit the ground, he kept hissing at me, as if to say, "There's more where that came from, tough guy." Blood dripped from my finger as I called over to the driver who was preparing to tow away my other truck.

"You ever hear of a lizard that looks like a dinosaur and tries to bite your finger off?"

"That there's an alligator lizard! You ain't never seen an alligator lizard? How the hell long you been living around here?"

Too long? Or not long enough? I didn't know anymore. I finished clearing the back of the truck and turned my attention to the cab. It too was crammed full of trash from floor to ceiling.

But I hadn't put it there, and couldn't figure out who had. Until, that is, an annoyed-looking pack rat poked his head out to see who was tampering with the mansion he had painstakingly constructed out of plastic bottles, drip irrigation tubing, pieces of paper and canvas, scraps of lumber, and even a couple of socket wrenches that had gone missing years ago.

He didn't like being displaced from his home either, but put up less resistance than the alligator lizard. As he sullenly skulked off into the woods, I felt a twinge of sympathy. A look at my own living quarters would reveal that he and I had more in common than I would have liked to admit.

A disadvantage of owning a house bigger than you need is that it's easy to get into the habit of hanging onto everything, a habit to which I'd clearly succumbed. At least two rooms, the one where the band used to practice and the spare bedroom I'd turned into a library, had become little more than storage spaces and de facto dumping grounds.

There were hundreds of records, tapes and CDs, thousands of old copies of *Lookout*, and enough books to fill at least a dozen boxes. I knew what to do with the books and records: nearly all, even some that were quite valuable, disappeared for

pennies on the dollar into the second-hand shops of Berkeley.
I dumped boxes of cassettes, flyers, and fanzines onto the floor
at Gilman for the punks to rummage through. Most of the old
Lookouts went, sadly, to the recycling center.

More problematic was half a lifetime's worth of keepsakes,
memorabilia, souvenirs, knick-knacks, and trinkets. Some had
intrinsic value, but far more numerous were things—posters,
maps, ticket stubs, a 1976 guide to visiting the Eiffel Tower—
that held only sentimental worth, and often not much of that.

I built a massive bonfire at the bottom of the driveway.
Into it went most of the aforementioned items, along with love
letters, financial records, and bags of clothing, some dating back
to the disco era and so un-stylish that not even the Salvation
Army would touch them.

The sofa—the one the bear had napped on after his ram-
page through my kitchen—went to my sister. The table, around
which the family had celebrated Christmases and Thanksgivings
in the long-ago 1980s, wound up with my mother, along with a
couple other pieces of furniture. Everything else went to thrift
stores or into the flames.

Things that wouldn't burn—foreign coins, costume jewelry
left over from my glam rock days, colored glass, stones and
seashells I'd dragged home from my travels—I scattered across
the fields and forest. Years, even centuries hence, I hoped,
someone would puzzle over how a 1939 World's Fair medallion,
an Icelandic 100 kroner piece, or a volcanic rock from Death
Valley had found its way into the Spy Rock wilderness.

If I'd stopped to think about every object I parted with
during those final weeks, I'd still be taking inventory today.
Instead, I moved quickly, decisively, not allowing myself to stop
and reminisce. My footsteps sounded more loudly through the
house as one room after another was emptied out.

Poking through the ashes of my bonfire, I felt raw and ravaged, as if years of scabbed-over emotions had been ripped away. Yet at the same time, I felt lighter and freer than I had in ages. A neighbor drove up, curious about my comings and goings, not to mention the great clouds of smoke that had been rising into the sky for the past day and a half.

On hearing I was preparing to sell the place, he instantly offered to buy it. I told him I wasn't ready to put it on the market yet, that I first wanted to restore the house to something resembling its former beauty. He said there was no need for that, he'd take it as it was. Well, that was easy, I thought, and we shook hands on the deal.

Though I no longer had to, I kept working anyway. I polished the walls, the woodwork, the floors, and cupboards until they seemed to glow from deep within. I cleaned the windows till they sparkled, pulled the curtains away to let light come flooding through. Standing back to admire my handiwork, I couldn't help being reminded of the Edward Hopper painting, "Sun in an Empty Room."

My friend John K. Samson, from the Canadian band The Weakerthans, has written a song about that painting and the haunting, aching nostalgia it evokes for a place no longer lived in. The chorus, a repeated refrain of the title phrase, echoes relentlessly through my mind every time I recall my last lingering look at the home that would never again be mine.

I made a final survey of the land, retracing well-worn paths, stopping in familiar places to gaze out over the canyons, fields, and forests, at the far-flung Yolla Bollys arching their backs against the eastern sky. Behind me, the ridge, its crest serrated with rich, dark firs, flowed into the stolid, implacable mass of Iron Peak, crowned by the long-abandoned lookout tower that had lent its name and inspiration to so many of my endeavors.

Over the years, the magnificent had been rendered mundane by time and habitude, but the act of leaving seemed to endow my surroundings with greater power and majesty than I'd ever managed to notice before. I was leaving Spy Rock, but, I wondered, would Spy Rock ever leave me?

It hasn't yet.

I can't cut up some strawberries without drifting back to that cocoon-like kitchen, where I stood at the window looking out over the land from which I'd harvested my dinner. I can't see a just-past-new moon impaled on one of Manhattan's spires without recalling a time when that slender crescent was the brightest object in the sky.

For much of my life, beginning long before I came to the mountain, I'd practiced the Chinese martial art of t'ai chi. But I never quite grasped the concept of *yun shou,* "move hands like clouds," until I watched the clouds wrap themselves around the top of Iron Peak. To this day I can scarcely move my hands at all without remembering that sight.

As I was finishing my stroll around the land, the sun slipped behind the ridge. The gathering shade ushered in a slight breeze, enough to stir to life a few bedraggled wind chimes still dangling from the trees. My vision blurred, and the sounds of creaking branches, rustling leaves, and wistful birdcalls receded beyond perception.

There would be other adventures, further epiphanies, more arrivals back where I had once belonged, but I wondered, questioned, doubted whether I would ever again encounter the serenity and serendipity, the sense of purpose and place that I found at the end of Spy Rock Road.

I stepped out of the house and took one last breath of Spy Rock air, the scents and vapors, fragrances and dust motes, that had for so long shaped and colored my life. Then, breathing out twenty-two years of love, isolation, tragedy, accomplishment, loneliness, triumph, rage, and transcendence, 1 turned away, closing the door behind me.

Larry Livermore was born in Detroit and arrived in California in 1968. He was the editor and publisher of *Lookout* magazine, the co-founder of Lookout Records, and a longtime columnist for *Maximum Rocknroll* and *Punk Planet*. A contributor to numerous other magazines, books, and anthologies, he has also sung and played guitar for the Lookouts and the Potatomen. He lives in Brooklyn.

Read more of Larry's work at www.larrylivermore.com.

Gabrielle Bell (cover art) was born in London and grew up on Spy Rock. Her books include *Lucky, Cecil and Jordan in New York*, and *The Voyeurs*. She lives in Brooklyn.